DILLINGER AT WORK

One man remained outside at the wheel of the car while Dillinger and one other entered the bank. John was carrying a trombone case containing a machine gun. Once inside, he opened the case and pointed the weapon while his companion began looting the money cages.

Police, called by an alarm, swarmed outside the door.

Dillinger ordered his aide to get all the money. "We'll kill these coppers and get away. Take your time."

A burst of machine-gun fire killed one policeman. The outlaws' blue Plymouth roared away, bullets chasing it.

It was found abandoned the next day, full of bullet holes and bloodstains, but of the men and money there was no trace.

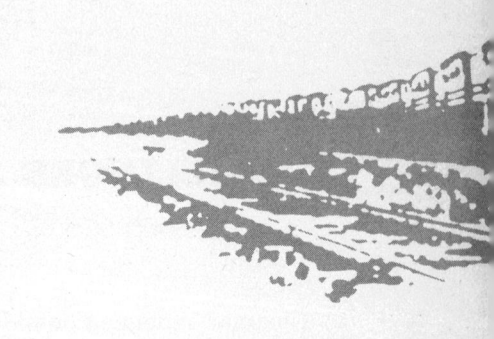

THE ILLUSTRATED HISTORY
OF GANGS FROM
JESSE JAMES TO MURPH THE SURF

GANGS and GANGSTERS

by HANK MESSICK
and BURT GOLDBLATT

BALLANTINE BOOKS • NEW YORK

Copyright © 1974 by Hank Messick and Burt Goldblatt
All rights reserved under International and
Pan-American Copyright Conventions.
SBN 345-23897-4-200
First Printing: April, 1974
Design and layout by Burt Goldblatt
Cover photo by Burt Goldblatt
Printed in the United States of America

BALLANTINE BOOKS
A Division of Random House, Inc.
201 East 50th Street, New York, N.Y. 10022

For Paul S. Messick, an old cowboy
and
Robert and Selma Cohen, who reach out

Contents

	Introduction	1
	Prologue—Then and Now	3
1	Jesse James Had a Wife	9
2	Go Home and Die	51
3	Blind White Devils	91
4	He Lost It at the Movies	121
5	Old Creepy was a Thief	157
6	Impossible Dreamers	187
	About the Authors	210
	Acknowledgments and Picture Credits	211
	Index	212

> *Ironically, in view of the FBI's reputation, the gangs of the 1930s, led by John Dillinger, Alvin Karpis, and the like, were more closely related to Jesse James than to the crime syndicates even then gaining power and influence.*
> —The Mobs and the Mafia

Introduction

IN THE LAWLESS nature of things there is first what might be called "unorganized crime." Next comes "disorganized crime" and, finally, "organized crime." This last, for all practical purposes, would appear to be broad enough to include the ultimate sophistication, despite the fact that not long ago Canadian police officials came up with an additional refinement—"syndicated crime." Thus inspired, the Canadians were able to insist that while, alas, organized crime was well established in the Dominion, there was happily no evidence of sinister, made-in-U.S. syndicated crime. Objective observers, however, disagreed with both the conclusion and the logic by which it was reached. The Canadian attitude resembled rationalizations of politicians in U.S. cities who, over the years, protected homegrown gangsters on the grounds that they keep syndicate hoods out of town. Ah Louisville!

While definitions are of necessity somewhat arbitrary, one can begin in this fashion:

Unorganized Crime—lawless activity by individuals.

Disorganized Crime—lawless activity by gangs.

Organized Crime—lawless activity by cartels or syndicates.

Obviously these are simplifications. Much more is involved. In a companion volume, *The Mobs and the Mafia,* the authors defined organized crime as "a continuing conspiracy to gain money and power without regard for law by utilizing economic and physical force, public and private corruption, in an extension of the free-enterprise system."

One can easily see why the crimes of individuals would not fall within this definition. The key word is "conspiracy." Individuals acting alone are not engaged in a conspiracy. Similarly, the key word for criminal activity by gangs is "continuous."

Gangs operate on a specific mission basis. There is no continuous conspiracy. The same gang may reassemble later to rob another bank, but there is no organizational life in the interim between jobs. Only the leadership remains constant. Jesse James or John Dillinger seldom used the same team on successive jobs. Each team was organized to meet the needs of that job. When a gang leader is killed or captured the gang ceases to be. Its members may reappear in other gangs under other leaders or may start a gang of their own. Contrast this to syndicate operations where when the boss is jailed we are assured by the press that he is continuing to run the mob from prison and when he dies there are a dozen eager lieutenants to step into his shoes.

Since this book is to be concerned with disorganized crime we should perhaps define that phenomenon as "an occasional conspiracy to gain money and fame (notoriety) without regard for law by utilizing physical force and public sympathy in less sophisticated acts of free enterprise."

Should anyone quarrel with "fame" as a motivating factor, they should be reminded that a bandit as primitive as Jesse James handed out a prepared press release when he robbed the Iron Mountain express on January 15, 1874. He even supplied the headline:

Most Daring Train Robbery On Record

In a work of limited size it is, of course, impossible to describe all the gangs, heroic or otherwise, which have spiced our history. Honesty also requires a word of caution: the reporting of disorganized crime is no better than the reporting of organized crime. Both bring to mind the words of Sidney J. Harris: " 'History' is gossip presented as fact." Nevertheless, this study with all its unavoidable defects may once again permit us to see the forest as well as the trees and allow us to isolate a few facts of sociological importance. That Jesse James rode a horse while Dillinger drove a car isn't all that significant. After all, both horse and car were usually stolen.

Prologue—Then and Now

CATTLE GRAZE TODAY on the site of the old courthouse at Pinelevel where once the legendary Sarasota Gang was indicted en masse for murder. A few score bricks near giant live oaks mark the old building, but of the town of Pinelevel which surrounded it there is no trace.

Once a rival of Tombstone for unrestrained violence, Pinelevel was located in central Florida some fifty miles east of the Gulf of Mexico. It was founded in the 1850s near the spot where Horse Creek flows into Peace River. The Seminole Wars were over and the area offered fertile land occupied by deer, black panthers, and armadillos. Spanish moss dripped from centuries-old cypress trees along rivers full of bass and alligators.

Quickly a cattle industry developed and the first of the millions of citrus trees that now perfume the spring air with the smell of orange blossoms were planted. Pinelevel was designated as county seat of a county that reached from the gulf on the west to Lake Okeechobee on the east. By 1880 it boasted two churches, several stores, warehouses, and scores of saloons in addition to the courthouse-jail. One historian has noted that there were "fourteen times as many saloons as any other business."

The county was too large for effective law enforcement, however, and too isolated. In the years following the Civil War it became headquarters for a gang as wild as any that rode the western ranges. From the little town, the gang rode forth to raid banks and stores along the Gulf Coast. Sarasota was the closest town and so often was it hit that the town's name was applied to the gang.

It was a large outfit, numbering at times as many as fifty members, and it had alliances with state politicians who were

Top, Peace River, overgrown and wild, near the old site of Pinelevel, Florida. *Right*, Hank Messick at Pinelevel site.

busily selling more than ten million acres of Florida land at the magnificent price of twenty-five cents an acre. On the eve of the Civil War, the land had been pledged by the state as security for railroad bonds. It was regained when the railroads defaulted and state officials moved quickly to take advantage of the potential bonanza. The outlaw gang served as something of an unofficial police force in quieting protests from "squatters" on the land.

Most notorious of the several leaders of the gang was a man known as "the Rattler." Legend had it that he was as deadly as a striking rattlesnake with his six-guns and as effective as an alligator with his knife. Even today, however, his true name isn't mentioned in the area, for his great-grandchildren are prosperous citizens. Respectable, too.

Public opinion tolerated the gang for years but even Pinelevel citizens were outraged when the gang kidnapped the postmaster of Sarasota and another man and took them, literally, for a ride. Their bodies were dumped in the palmetto bushes with bullets in their backs. The double murder was believed to have been politically inspired—the dead men were allegedly informers for a legislative committee seeking information on land deal shenanigans.

Twenty members of the gang were rounded up in Pinelevel and indicted for murder. Pending trial they were lodged in the county jail. One by one the prisoners escaped. By court day only nine remained. Newsmen from New York, Boston, and Chicago were on hand for the trial despite certain hardships. All stories had to be sent by oxcart to the nearest telegraph office at Tampa—some one hundred miles away. And liquor and beer had to come in from Sarasota—fifty miles away. A wagon train broke down near Myakka City at one point, forcing the press to turn to locally made homebrew.

In the end all but two members of the gang were acquitted. One promptly decamped through a hole in the roof of the jail, leaving a polite note of thanks for the jailer's hospitality. The second man was sentenced to hang, but that sentence was soon commuted to life imprisonment. Actually, he served three years before being pardoned. In 1961 he died at Fort Meyers, a wealthy and respected citizen.

If the effort to bring law and order to Pinelevel wasn't too successful, there were changes in the wind that would soon tame the town. Two years after the trial, Manatee County was split.

DeSoto sheriff Frank E. Cline, center, checks a 750-gallon moonshine still, raided near the old Pinelevel site.

Pinelevel became the seat of newly created DeSoto County. It was named after the Spanish explorer who, allegedly, first discovered that Peace River was a graveyard of prehistoric bones. Two years after DeSoto County was created, the booming town of Arcadia on the east bank of Peace River was designated county seat.

The years passed, the people of Pinelevel moved away. The buildings decayed. Pinelevel became a ghost town, and then not even that. The buildings were torn down as orange groves were planted. Today only Pinelevel Church remains—and the cemetery that was once boot hill. Far from a main road, there is not even the sound of an automobile to break the silence.

But the peace that hangs so heavily is sometimes broken. In mid-1973, the present sheriff of DeSoto County, Frank E. Cline, discovered a marijuana field growing on the banks of Horse Creek near the site of Pinelevel. The field was put under observation. A few nights later word came from the watching deputies that the tranquility of old Pinelevel was being disturbed by a wild "pot party." Cars were coming in from all kinds of "foreign" places.

Sheriff Cline, a professional policeman and no politician, broke up the party. Forty-three youths were arrested on a variety of charges, and large quantities of "grass" and pills were seized.

It was just another night's work for the sheriff, who spends much of his time chasing cattle rustlers and raiding moonshine stills. Gangs still form—in Florida and across the nation—only to fade away and be replaced by others. The bass leap high in Peace River and new generations of young alligators sun themselves on the banks as history repeats itself.

The fleeting nature of fame was well illustrated in Dallas, Texas, in 1973, when a young John Dillinger faced trial for burglary. His attorney commented:

"I figure if the people of Texas could elect for its treasurer a fellow named Jesse James, the name wouldn't make any difference."

A reward poster of the period, with a Starr .44 percussion revolver, one of Jesse James's favorite weapons.

1

Jesse James Had a Wife

ST. VALENTINE'S DAY, 1866, and in Liberty, Missouri, the taste of snow rode the morning wind. George Wymore dressed quickly and hurried to his breakfast. It was almost eight o'clock and he had a class to meet at William Jewell College.

Shots sounded on the street outside as a troop of horsemen pounded by. Wymore didn't bother to look. The war was over, the infamous raider Quantrill was dead, and heroics by men whose time had passed didn't impress the young student. Let them shout and shoot as they pleased—he had more important things to think about.

In a less objective mood was Greenup Bird. The cashier of the Clay County Savings and Loan Association was just opening for business, assisted by his son, William, when four men walked in with drawn revolvers. Judging by the sounds from the street, a small army waited outside in reserve. It was shocking, unprecedented. The Birds were too stunned to protest. They reached for the ceiling when ordered to do so, and they scurried through the open door to the vault when the leader of the bandits commanded. There they stood aghast as the intruders cheerfully dumped gold coins, banknotes, and some worthless bonds into a common grain sack.

Leaving the Birds "caged" in the bank vault, the confident robbers raced out to their horses. Six riders who had been patrolling the street in military fashion wheeled to join them. With the grain sack dangling heavily from a saddle horn, the troop headed out of town.

Wymore, his mind on his classes, had left his house about the same instant the robbers left the bank. Preoccupied, he ignored the uproar until, abruptly, the charging horsemen were almost on top of him. Just in time he ran for cover. The men pounded by—but then, as if on impulse, one of the horsemen wheeled his mount. Playfully, as if shooting at a rabbit, he leveled his revolver and fired four quick shots at the running figure. And then he was gone.

The student fell on his face, blood from four bullet holes spilling out to warm the frozen earth. Examination later revealed that each of the wounds was fatal. Soon the snow came, a veritable blizzard, to cover the bloodstains and effectively end all pursuit of the killer and his crew.

In dying, young Wymore had become part of history. Not only was the Liberty caper the first bank robbery in America, but it was the first job pulled by a man who was to become a living legend—Jesse James.

While no one could prove that James, then an eighteen-year-old veteran of Quantrill's Raiders, fired the shots at Wymore, almost all historians assumed that he alone possessed such deadly skill. Moreover, some saw the shooting as a premeditated act designed to clothe the band in terror and thus grease the leather for future exploits.

Over the decades it has been popular to paint Jesse and his older brother, Frank, as Robin Hoods on horseback, and to blame their career in crime on a grassroots rebellion against vested interests in the form of the railroads. The truth, insofar as it can be discerned, is somewhat less romantic.

Jesse Woodson James was the son of a transplanted Kentucky preacher who settled in Missouri in 1842. He never knew his father, however, for two years after his birth in 1847, the Reverend Robert James abandoned his family and his ministry to seek gold in California. Shortly after arriving there he died.

Attractive widows were in demand on the frontier, however, and Zerelda James soon remarried. It didn't work out, perhaps because another Kentuckian happened along. In any event she soon divorced her second husband to marry Dr. Reuben Samuels and, in doing so, achieved stability if nothing more. The marriage lasted.

Alexander Franklin James, four years older than Jesse, joined the Confederate Army at age sixteen when the Civil War began. Eventually, Frank ended up with Quantrill and rode with him to Lawrence, Kansas, where 142 people were murdered in a massacre that shocked both North and South. Jesse was too young for that expedition, but he learned something of the methods being used by both sides when Union soldiers visited

Top, the James home near Kearney, Missouri. The rear portion is the original house in which Frank and Jesse were born. *Above*, the original house.

Above, Charles Quantrill, who carved a bloody name for himself as the leader of a guerrilla band during the Civil War. *Below*, a Colt .44 navy percussion revolver, the type he carried.

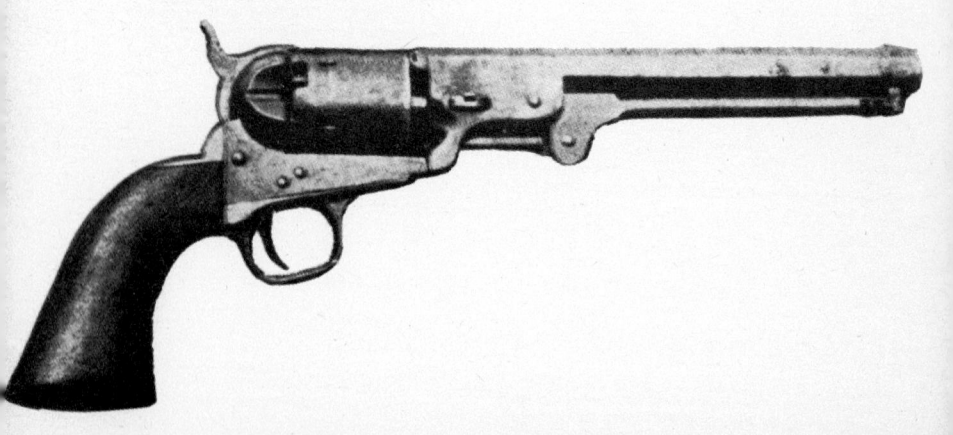

Above, Jesse James in 1864, riding with Quantrill at age seventeen. *Right*, Jesse at age twenty-three in 1870.

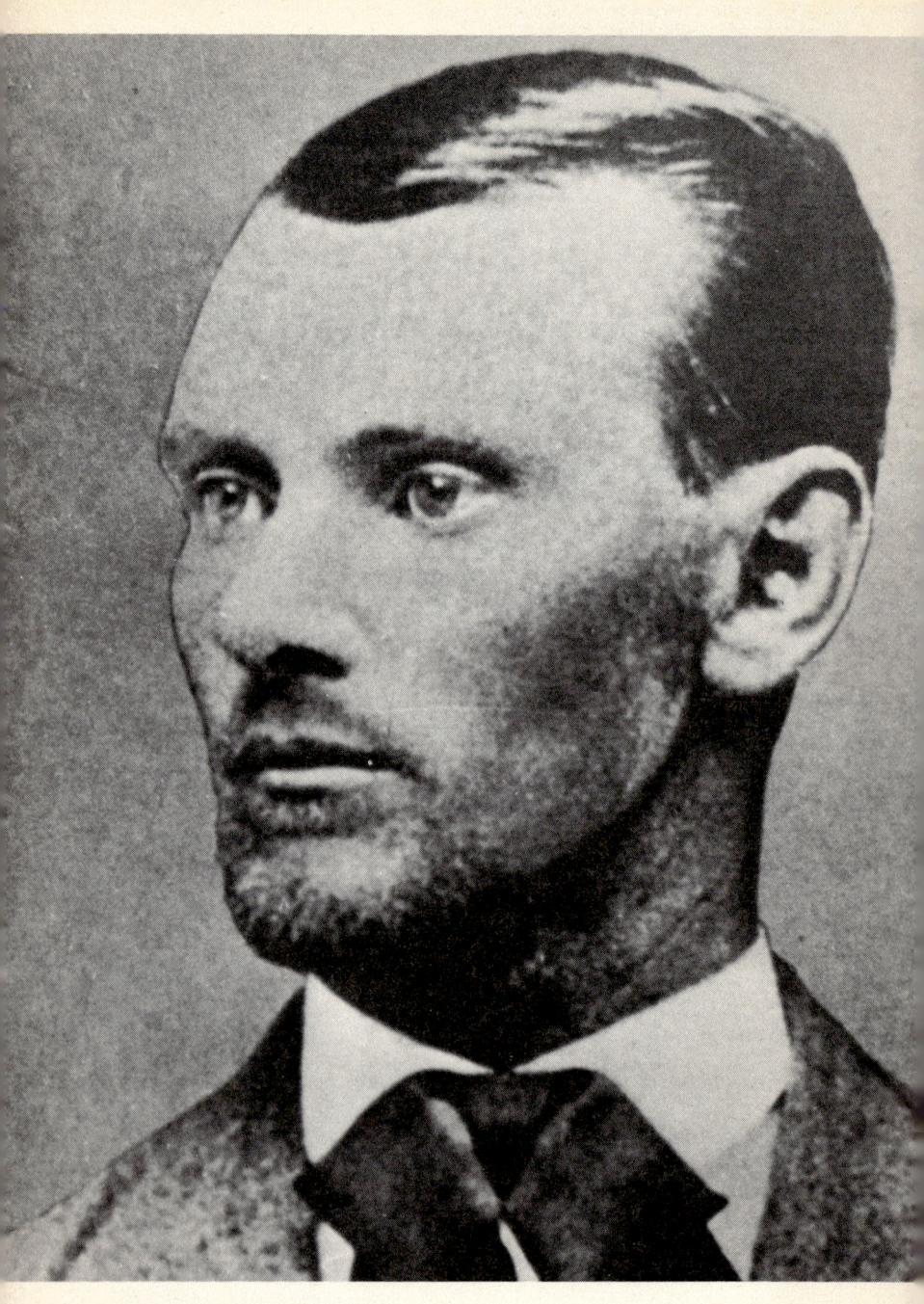

Jesse James, from a daguerreotype made in 1875 at Nebraska City, Nebraska.

his stepfather's farm and left the doctor dangling. Mrs. Samuels cut him down in time, and shortly thereafter moved to Rulo, Nebraska, on the Missouri River. Upon turning sixteen, Jesse rode off on a stolen horse to join his brother and Quantrill. His first assignment was to dress like a girl and lure sex-starved Union soldiers into ambushes.

But behind the smooth cheeks and restless blue eyes was a force Quantrill recognized and respected. Soon the young recruit was an officer, commanding older men. Among those gladly obeying him was his brother. For even among the guerrillas, Jesse James stood out as a man without fear, without pity, and without regret. He learned to kill casually, and to hold no man and no institution in awe.

One can attribute this development to many things, but, in essence, James was a man for the times. There had been little law and order as the frontier crept westward and there was less as the Civil War "legitimized" bandit activity. Men could kill and rob and call themselves patriots just as a century later right-wing Americans could praise organized murder in Indochina as a defense of freedom. The formal surrender of Robert E. Lee did not end the conflict for many west of the Mississippi. There the battle had been more personal, a struggle of neighbor against neighbor, family against family. Deeply rooted in the population of Missouri, Kansas, Texas, and Arkansas was the clan spirit brought from Scotland and carried westward by such pioneers as Daniel Boone and David Crockett. In later years much would be made of the Mafia code of "omerta," but in reality the tradition of loyalty, of protecting friends and kin, belonged to no national or ethnic group and was practiced in the Bad Lands of Missouri long before it was to become a badge of honor in the jungles of Manhattan. And the bloody battles that resulted rivaled the later vendettas within the Mafia, even if they got less attention from sociologists. Publicity-wise, the gunman on horseback came out even with his city counterpart for the dime novels of the Wild West were no more inaccurate than the lurid tales of La Cosa Nostra that became bestsellers a hundred years later.

The men who took orders from Jesse James did so because they recognized a leader, a godfather, who would supply some direction and purpose to their lives. He won their respect with his brains, and their affection with his courage and his skill. Six of them survived the war and rode with him to surrender.

Outside Lexington, Missouri, on April 15, 1865, they met a superior force of Union soldiers. Ignoring the white flag James carried, the Federal troops opened fire. Jesse's horse was killed and he was hit in the right lung. As his companions fled, James ran for a patch of deep woods. The main body of the enemy pursued the retreating guerrillas but several men followed the wounded man into the woods. It was a mistake. Gripping his revolver in both hands, James shot down the leading horseman and badly wounded another. The others said to hell with it and rode back to their companions. After all, the war *was* over.

The fallen leader was rescued and, still near death, was passed from ex-guerrilla to ex-guerrilla until he reached his mother's home in the Nebraska Territory. There his stepfather, Dr. Samuels, treated him. By August he was able to travel and the family boarded a steamboat for the return to Missouri. Near Kansas City he was left with an uncle while his stepfather went on to Clay County. It was for James a uniquely happy time for he came under the personal care of a cousin, a pretty young girl. Nine years passed before he could marry her but—at least according to legend—he was a faithful lover both before and after marriage. Unlike many bad men and wise guys, he felt no need to boost his ego by seducing every women he met.

When able to ride, James kissed his girl and headed for the family farm near Liberty. In the next few weeks he assembled his gang. Some like Cole and Jim Younger, Wood and Clarence Hite, were cousins. There was brother Frank, of course, and other ex-guerrillas such as George and Oliver Shepherd, Tom Little, and Andy McGuire. All had enjoyed the reckless, ruthless life with Quantrill, and to a man they flinched from the idea of becoming sodbusters. If they had any goal beyond freedom to do as they pleased, it was to settle down some day on a huge spread littered with fat cows and fast horses and there to found a personal empire so powerful it would command respect from all. But there was no hurry, these young men thought, for life however harsh it seemed today offered excitement and opportunity enough.

The bank at Liberty was their first project and its success encouraged them immensely. Perhaps the fact that no one in Liberty would go on record as identifying the bandits was most satisfactory. Fear was at work—a fear one still encounters in rural communities and city slums today. One may finger a stranger without hesitation, but it takes a brave man to send a

Above, Frank James in 1865 at age twenty-two. *Right*, Frank in 1871, age twenty-eight. *Below*, Mrs. Samuels with Frank and Jesse.

native son to prison when behind him he leaves loyal friends and relatives. But, unfortunately, one can only rob the hometown bank so many times. Sooner or later it becomes necessary to venture far afield where the natives might be downright hostile. Five gang members, "on their own," attempted to rob a bank in Savannah, Missouri, and were driven off when the owner of the bank seized his gun and started shooting. Properly humble, the five confessed their error to their leader and were readmitted.

As if to demonstrate the proper method of liberating a town's cash, James soon led fourteen men against a bank in Richmond, Missouri. Yelling and shooting, the band stirred up the dust on May 23, 1867, and got away with several thousand dollars. But it wasn't easy. Citizens shot back. A pitched battle developed. The mayor was killed but no raider was even wounded. Made arrogant by the smell of gunpowder, the James gang tried to break open the jail to free some of their friends. They failed, killing the jailer and his young son in the attempt. This time when the outlaws fled they left behind outrage and armed men on their trail. In an effort to confuse the pursuers, the gang split up. The James boys and their cousins kept riding hard, but

Jesse's mother, Zerelda Samuels—note her armless right sleeve.

some of the other men stopped to rest. Payne Johnson was almost cornered in a farm house one rainy night, but he escaped into the woods after firing both barrels of a shotgun. The blast killed a little girl and a member of the posse. Two other men were less fortunate. Captured while sleeping, they were immediately lynched. Still another member of the gang was safely arrested and taken to jail to stand trial. A mob gathered quickly and hung him to a tree. It was a nasty affair all around.

A year passed, tempers cooled, and the loot was spent. Unwilling to arouse Missouri to anger again, James led his men to Kentucky and there on May 20, 1868, they robbed the bank at Russellville. There was quite a bit of shooting but the gang got away with $14,000 in loot and the pursuers soon lost their trail in the woods.

The Kentucky caper proved its value. Few people at the time connected it with the previous robberies in Missouri. As more months passed without a new outrage, people relaxed. Out of sight, out of mind. And to allow the sleeping dogs more time to dream, James waited another eighteen months. In the interim some members of the gang took trips—to Mexico and California. Perhaps they were seeking their dream ranch, or maybe they

Mrs. Jesse James, with some of her husband's weapons.

Cole (*left*) and Jim Younger, before Cole joined Quantrill.

Top left, John Younger; *right*, Cole Younger. *Bottom left*, Jim Younger; *right*, Bob Younger.

wanted freedom to spend their loot without attracting comment from neighbors who knew they had never done an honest day's work. But even when on pleasure bent, an executive cannot help but make notes. Jesse found the busy railroads a thought-provoking phenomena.

When Jesse struck again he changed his modus operandi. Whether he had become overconfident or had decided that excessive force provoked excessive reaction isn't clear, but in any case he took along only his brother, Frank, and his cousin, Cole Younger, to Gallatin, Missouri on December 7, 1869. The robbery went off smoothly enough until Jesse lost his temper. The cashier could come up with only $700. The disappointed bandit promptly shot him through the head. Until then no shot had been fired, no alarm given. But, thanks to the James boys, the robbery of a bank no longer seemed incredible. The moment the shot was heard, the citizens of the small town understood its implications. By the time Jesse and Cole reached the horses which Frank was holding, the counterattack had begun. Frightened by the volley of shots, the shouts of alarm, Jesse's horse reared and threw the outlaw who had one foot in the stirrup.

Somehow, Jesse got his foot clear and his brother rode back through the bullet-filled dust to help. Jesse scrambled erect, then vaulted to the horse's rump behind Frank and away they went. A posse formed quickly in expectation of easily catching the overloaded horse, but Jesse was a horse thief as well as a bank robber and just outside of town he helped himself to a good animal. Escape after that was routine.

But the aftermath wasn't routine. If the forces of law and order—well, anyway, order—didn't have the killer of the cashier, they had his horse. And, by a bit of rural detective work equal to the later exploits of the FBI, the horse was traced to its rightful owner. When investigators approached the family farm in Clay County, Frank and Jesse—obviously tipped—thundered out of the barn on horseback. The usual volley of shots was fired with the usual results. This time, however, the truth was no longer the secret of the closemouthed folks of Clay County. The James boys were identified and the legend began to build.

Again, however, there was a pause to let the heat die, to spend the loot. It was June 3, 1871, before the gang struck again and this time they ranged far afield to Corydon, Iowa. Taking advantage of a political meeting which had drawn much of the

Bob, Jim, and Cole Younger, with sister Henrietta Younger, in 1889.

town's population, the bandits had little trouble in collecting $45,000—their biggest haul to date. According to legend, Jesse rode by the speaker's platform after the robbery and politely suggested that when they found the time they might care to untie the cashier back at the bank.

Three other robberies followed—two in 1872 and another on May 23, 1873. By then Jesse was convinced it was time to diversify. For several years he had been thinking about it, testing men and techniques. Suddenly he decided to do it—rob a train.

The first train robbery in history—so at least say the historians—occurred just west of Cincinnati on May 8, 1865. The bandits, all unknown, stopped the train by piling crossties on the rails. Then they escaped across the Ohio River to Kentucky, a practice that in time would make the Newport-Covington area famous as "Little Mexico."

Indiana was the scene of the next train robbery on October 6, 1866. Two men boarded at Seymour, much in the fashion of modern-day skyjackers, donned masks, and ambled into the unlocked express car. When they had collected the loot, some $13,000, they signaled the engineer to stop, then dived overboard into the darkness.

The so-called "Reno Gang" was blamed, the gang consisting of some brothers named Reno and assorted cousins. It had a short career. After pulling several more jobs, one group was arrested near Cincinnati and another some one hundred miles down the Ohio at New Albany. A mob of self-styled vigilantes broke into the New Albany jail, confiscated the gangsters, and hung them to the nearest tree. Fearing something similar might happen in Cincinnati, officials put their prisoners on a train and headed them back to Indiana to stand trial. Undaunted, some law-and-order citizens took a leaf from the Reno Gang's book and boarded the train. Three prisoners were taken at gun point and promptly strung up.

All of which was not exactly a good precedent, perhaps, but Jesse James was supremely confident that he could play with trains and get away with it even as he had done with banks. Especially inviting was the information that vast shipments of gold were being sent east by train on a regular basis. This practice continued over the years, reaching a climax in August, 1892, when a train left San Francisco with $20 million in gold coins

Chicago Daily

SATURDAY, AUGUST ... 1893—SIXTEEN PAGES

AS SECRET AS NIGHT.

TRANSCONTINENTAL SHIPMENT OF $20,000,000 IN GOLD.

Unknown Train on an Unknown Road in Care of an Unknown Express Company Speeding Across the Country from San Francisco to the East Loaded with Wealth from the United States Sub-treasury—Precautions Taken to Prevent Information Being Made Public.

Five of the heaviest and strongest postal cars, bearing $20,000,000 in gold coin, left San Francisco Aug. 4, and are now speeding over the rails towards Chicago as fast as steam can carry them, on the way to their destination in ———. The train is guarded by forty of the ——— clerks of the United States mail service, the shipment being in charge of Capt. James E. White of Washington.

It is no easy ——— to transport $20,000,000 in gold coin the entire length of the country. It is, perhaps, the heaviest shipment ever started on an overland tour in the United States. Therefore the greatest secrecy was necessary, and it has been maintained by the government officials in charge.

Supt. Troy of the Railway Mail Service several days ago started West with thirteen clerks of the local mail service, several clerks from Cleveland, and before he arrived in San Francisco he had selected enough men along the line to make up the entire number which was to guard Uncle Sam's treasure.

So well did Supt. Troy guard his mission that the chosen clerks themselves did not know where they were going until just as they

Those of them who were ———

Chicago

TUESDAY, AUGUST

DID NOT WAIT LONG.

"GOLD TRAIN" TARRIES IN CHICAGO THIRTY-FOUR MINUTES.

If Guards and Employes Had Been Deaf, Dumb, and Blind They Could Not Have Told Less Anent the Trip and the Train's Valuable Freight than They Did—Description of the Cars That Held the $20,000,000 in Yellow Coin—Armed Guards Look Tired—Those on Board.

The train bearing the $20,000,000 in gold coin being transferred from the San Francisco subtreasury to the one in New York City passed through Chicago yesterday morning. It rolled into the Sixteenth street switching yards of the Burlington road at 8:25 a. m., pulled into the Lake Shore and Michigan Southern Depot at 8:40, and ten minutes later was on its way to New York, where it should arrive today.

The officials in charge of the transfer have endeavored to keep every movement secret, and the arrival and departure of the train in ——— from the principal cities en ———

The newspaper reports of the $20,000,000 gold shipment as it passed through Chicago.

A letter sent to the *Police Gazette* by Jesse James.

The James Gang in a train holdup (a contemporary sketch).

and forty armed guards. But by 1892, James was no longer a problem.

Word came that a Rock Island train due to pass through Adair, Iowa, on July 21, 1873, would be carrying $75,000 in gold. John Rafferty was at the throttle. According to some historians, apparently possessed of unusual powers, Rafferty rode with "his heart glad that the grain harvest was to be good for the struggling farmers." Be that as it may, the train rounded a curve, its headlight bouncing off the fields of wheat and corn. Up ahead, the James boys tugged on a rope attached to a rail, pulling the rail out of place. Rafferty, alerted too late, slammed on the brakes, but the engine plowed on off the rails and overturned. Like another more famous railroad man, Rafferty was scalded to death by steam. The fireman was burned and several passengers were injured.

Firing revolvers and whooping—the same style used in bank jobs—the gangsters came out of the bushes and deprived the passengers of their valuables. All the loot went into the conventional grain sacks. Meanwhile, other robbers cleaned out the express car, but the safe held only about $3,500, instead of the treasure expected. It developed that the gold had been shipped earlier on another train.

If, however, the haul was less than expected, the value to Jesse's legend was immeasurable. As a bankrobber he might win some grudging admiration for his daring, but he could never hope to be a hero. The bank was too important to the ordinary man and woman, too personal. The railroads were another matter, however. Vast and impersonal, with control exercised by faceless men back east, the railroads were generally hated. Through their political influence in Congress, they had been given millions of acres of land throughout the West, and they used that land to control the lives of settlers. Moreover, the railroad brought industrialization, and it was to escape the factories that many men went west. As the flood of immigrants from central and southern Europe suddenly swelled to tidal-wave proportions, the anger of the "Old Americans" increased. That many of the newcomers were put to work building the railroads did little to soothe the bitterness, although it did help the Mafia get a firm base in Kansas City.

In any event, Jesse's image improved sharply when he began jousting with the railroads. Soon people were talking of Jesse as the man who "stole from the rich and gave to the poor." They could get quite specific. There was this poor, old widow woman—her name and address might vary from place to place —who offered the James boys hospitality when they needed it. Jesse sensed the woman was troubled in heart and, being a natural-born do-gooder, he persuaded her to tell her sad story. Seems the mortage was due on the broken-down old ranch and the Rich Man was coming that very day to foreclose. So Jesse promptly produced the necessary cash, then hid nearby as the happy widow paid off. When the Rich Man came riding by

Above, a Wells Fargo strong box. *Opposite page, left,* Frank James and wife; *right,* Jesse James and wife.

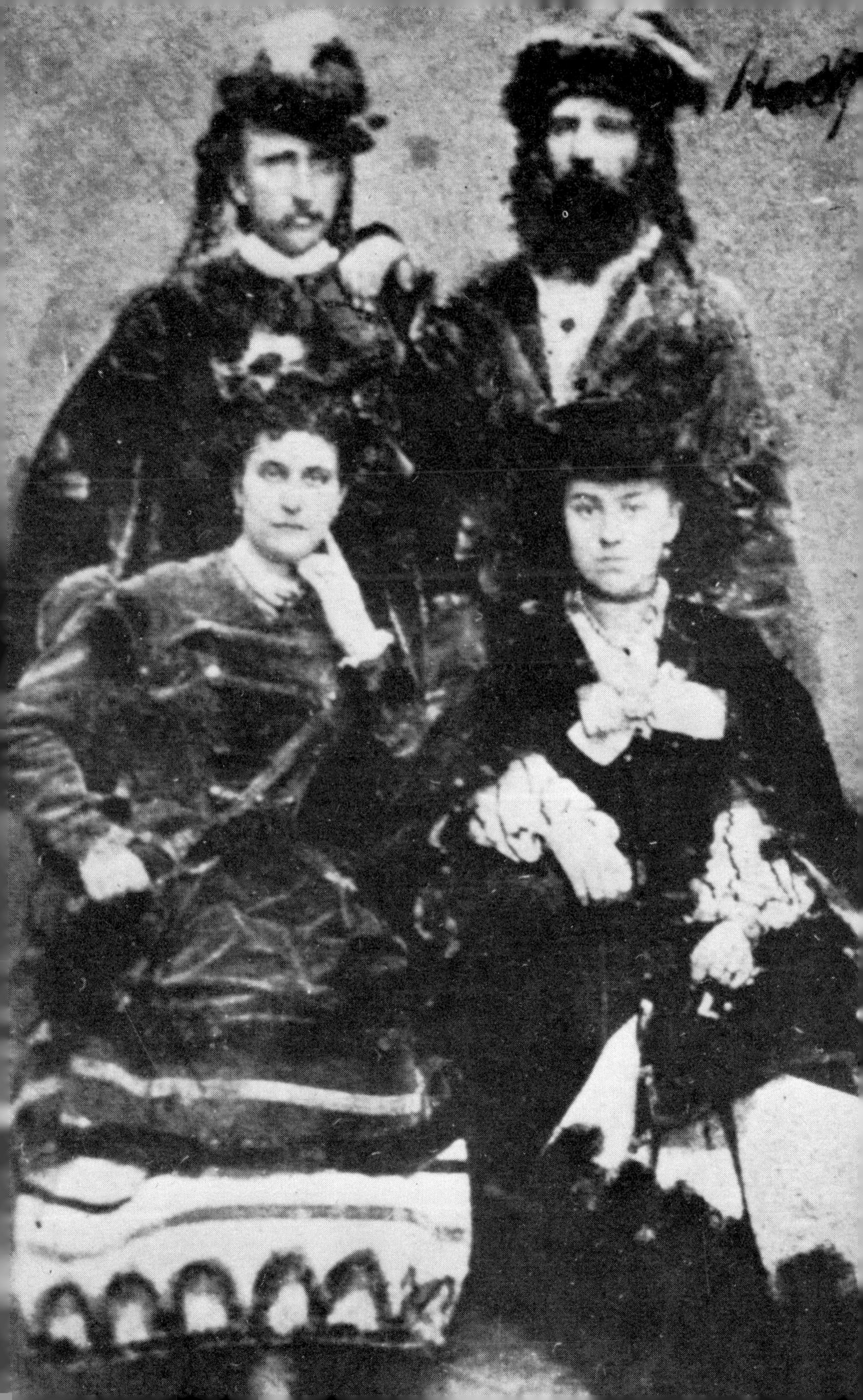

with the loot, Jesse promptly robbed him of it, and perhaps a little more for good measure, and vanished into the sunset with a happy heart.

After a stage robbery, just to prove his versatility, and another train job, Jesse apparently decided that he had proved himself sufficiently and could now take unto himself a wife. Zerelda Mimms, the cousin who had been named after his mother, was still waiting. They met in Kansas City at the home of a relative who also happened to be a minister. Dressed in black broadcloth and shining boots, Jesse was a handsome, romantic figure, and Zerelda was proud of him. From their union came two children, a boy and a girl. Jesse James, Jr. grew up to become a successful attorney in Kansas City.

Frank, as usual taking his lead from his younger brother, took the plunge as well. He eloped with Annie Ralston, a long-time girlfriend.

Both marriages endured until death did them part. But they did little to soften the two outlaws as the case of John W.

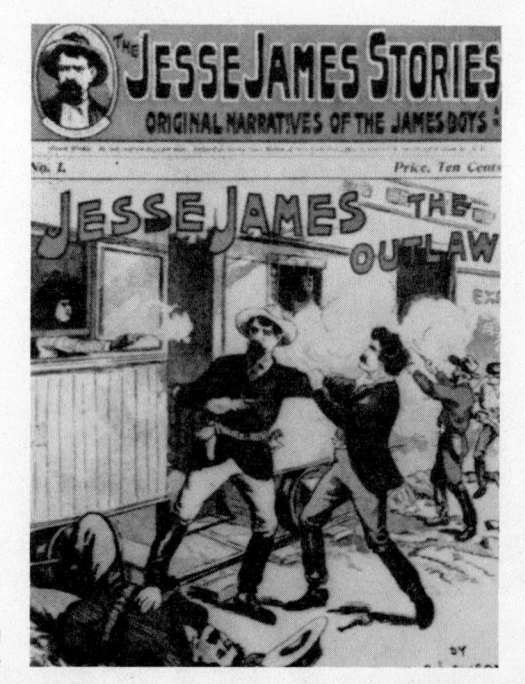

The magazines of the period kept the legends alive.

Whicher proved. A Pinkerton detective assigned to track down the gang, Whicher came down to Clay County from Chicago with a plan to go underground. He would change clothes and personality, become a country hick looking for work, and wander around freely until he could pick up a clue to the gang's whereabouts. Disregarding warnings from wiser men, he started walking toward the James family ranch some four miles from town. He found what he was seeking quickly—or, rather, it found him. Jesse James stepped out from behind a bush and took the visitor prisoner. The body was found next day, full of bullet holes. Hogs had eaten part of the face, but identification was made by a tattoo on his upper arm. Eventually the full story came out. The detective had been tortured in an effort to learn Pinkerton secrets. When he refused to talk, Jesse shot him through the heart and Frank through the head. Allegedly, it was his soft, uncalloused hands that convinced the outlaws that the stranger was no honest laborer.

On the same day that the detective's body was found, one

The cabin near Monegan Springs, Missouri, where the fatally wounded detective captain Louis Lull and deputy sheriff Daniels were carried after their gunfight with the Younger brothers, March 16, 1874. John Younger was killed in the fight, Jim wounded.

The James Boys and the Younger Brothers. *Back row, from left,* Cole and Bob Younger; *front row,* Jesse and Frank James.

of the four Younger brothers was shot down in the Ozark Mountains by another Pinkerton operative. With a colleague, he had located John and Jim Younger at one of their many hideouts. Both agents were fatally shot in the battle, but one lived long enough to tell the story. Unhurt was Jim Younger, who took time to bury his brother in an orchard before fleeing.

The Pinkerton National Detective Agency, regarded as the FBI of its day despite its private capacity, reacted sharply to the loss of three operatives. And when another secret agent reported in January, 1875, that the James boys were back at the family ranch, plans were made quickly. A special train brought a small army close to the ranch in the dead of night. The moon shone as men and horses disembarked on the frozen plains and the train moved quietly away. No alarm was given as the detectives surrounded the farmhouse. The only light from within came from the fireplace where coals glowed. Obviously, the occupants had retired.

So feared were the James boys, and so bitter were the Pinkertons, that no attempt was made to effect a surrender. Instead, a bomb-like device was tossed through a window. The explosion rocked the building. Mrs. Samuels, mother of Frank and Jesse James, discovered that her right arm had been blown off at the elbow. Eight-year-old Archie Samuels, half-brother of Jesse James, was fatally hurt, dying the same night. An old servant was seriously injured and Dr. Samuels was badly burned.

Jesse and Frank were unhurt—and for a good reason. The undercover spy had passed bad information. Neither man was at home that night.

Public opinion supported the outlaws and a bill to give them amnesty passed the Missouri legislature. Thanks to some technicalities, quickly uncovered, it never became law. The Pinkertons were forced to leave their agents unavenged. The James boys were now heroes in the public eye, bravely fighting the Establishment on behalf of the Little Man. And when they murdered the farmer who had sheltered the Pinkerton spy, the people approved. An eye for an eye, and a life for a life.

Had the James boys called it quits and hung up their guns at that point in time, odds are they could have settled down on a ranch in Texas and become both respectable and famous as pioneers and philanthropists. But the call of easy money was too strong, despite their new roles as family men. Instead of retiring, they began to roam wider: a train in Kansas that netted

A contemporary drawing of the James Gang holding up the Austin and San Antonio, Texas, stage. *Opposite page,* a reward poster of the period.

them $60,000, a stagecoach in Texas that brought in only $3,000 and another train in Missouri where $15,000 was taken. All in all, 1876 was a pretty good year, so the gang decided to climax the century anniversary of the United States by riding north to Minnesota and proving that free enterprise was profitable from border to border.

It was August when the troop reached Minnesota. Very leisurely, posing as civil engineers looking for railroad routes, they scouted the southern part of the state. In the party were the James brothers; Cole, Jim and Bob Younger; Charles Pitts, Clel Miller, and William Stiles. By September they had selected the college town of Northfield on the Cannon River as the target. On September 7 the raid took place. Jesse, Pitts, and Bob Younger lounged on the street near the First National Bank as the other men divided into two groups and got into position on Division Street to control the citizenry. At a signal from the outside men—yells and shots—Jesse led his companions into the bank where the cashier and two employees were at work. But, for once, James encountered civilians as determined not to yield as he was to have his way. Joseph L. Heywood refused

$25,000 REWARD
JESSE JAMES
DEAD OR ALIVE

$15,000 REWARD FOR FRANK JAMES

$5000 Reward for any Known Member of the James Band

SIGNED:
ST. LOUIS MIDLAND RAILROAD

to open the safe and even a knife at his throat—a slight wound was made—wouldn't change his mind. Ironically, the safe was already unlocked, although its door was closed. A futile shot was fired; then the angry robbers started grabbing up all the loose cash they could find at the cashier's window.

Meanwhile, outside, the citizens had rallied quickly. A young medical student, Henry M. Wheeler, was standing outside the Dampier House when the shooting started. He rushed inside, grabbed a breech-loading carbine of Civil War vintage, and ran to an upstairs window overlooking the street.

Inside the bank, Jesse decided it was time to leave. He glanced around as he reached the door. The indomitable Heywood, blood streaming from his throat and from bruises on his head where he had been pistol-whipped, reached his feet and was staggering toward a desk. James fired once and the cashier dropped with a bullet in his brain.

As the men dashed out of the bank, young Wheeler was getting acquainted with his borrowed gun. He narrowly missed Jim Younger. Correcting his aim, he put his next bullet through Miller, killing him almost instantly. By now other

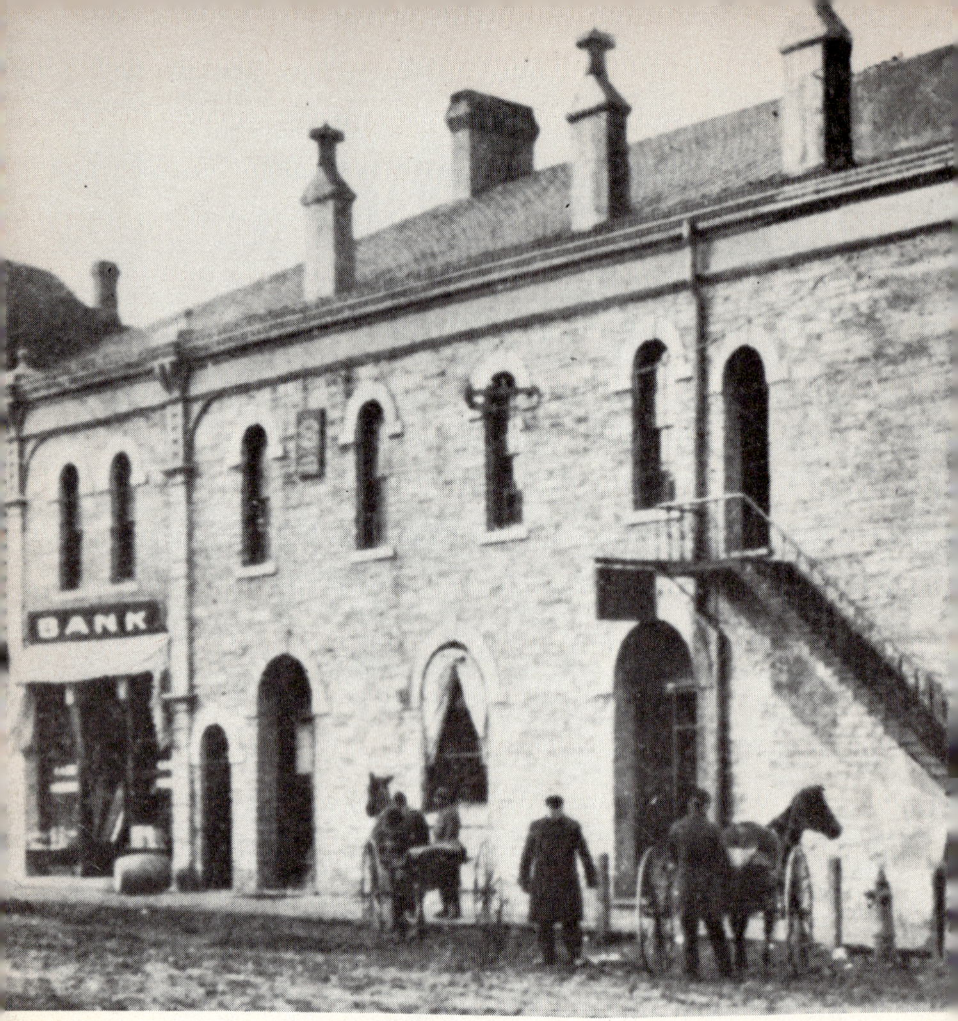
BANK

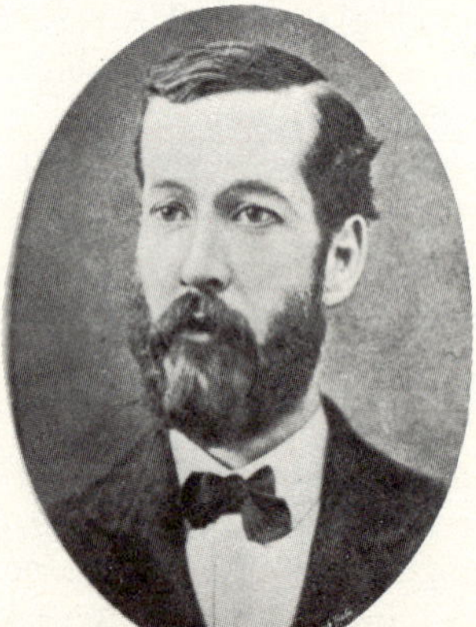

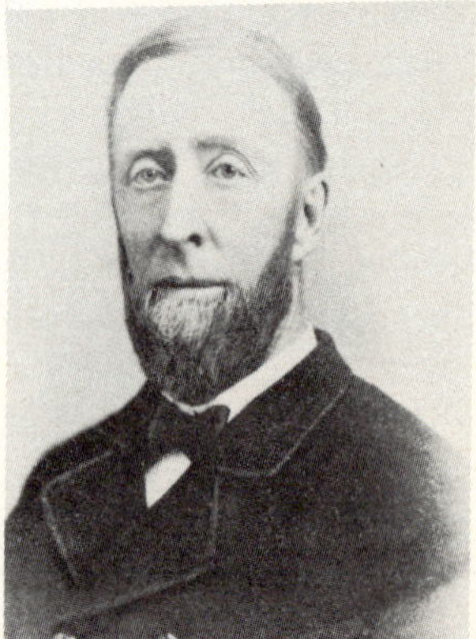

Top, the First National Bank of Northfield, Minnesota, in 1870. *Below, from left,* Joseph Lee Heywood, the murdered cashier; Henry M. Wheeler (taken years later); Anselm R. Manning, a merchant who fought the robbers.

citizens had seized firearms—ranging from shotguns to single-shot pistols—and joined the fight. The entire battle lasted less than seven minutes. When it ended two robbers were dead and the remaining six were wounded. In addition to Heywood, one townsman was killed and two wounded.

But the episode wasn't over. Quickly and efficiently the pursuit was organized. By telegraph the entire state was alerted, and the James Gang was hunted as never before. Minnesota citizens didn't share the romantic notions of their neighbors to the south, and Jesse could find no sanctuary. The flight became a nightmare with as many as a thousand men dogging the trail of the tired and wounded bandits.

Less than a week after the fisaco at Northfield, the gang was surrounded in a thick woods near Mankato. Allegedly, Jesse suggested that Cole Younger be put out of his misery inasmuch as he was going to die anyway and was hampering the retreat. The two relatively sound Youngers emphatically rejected the idea, and resented it. Then and there the gang broke up. Jesse and Frank in one group, the three Youngers and Pitts in the other. Early next morning the Youngers broke out of the trap and got away. The James boys followed suit the next night, although they had but one horse. They didn't have it long for in the darkness it was shot out from under them. The same bullet wounded Frank James near the knee and lodged in Jesse's thigh. Still the outlaws were able to run into a cornfield where no one dared follow in the dark. By next morning the fugitives had escaped, stolen two gray horses, and headed west. Pursuit lasted until the border of Dakota Territory was reached on September 17, ten days after the holdup. Dodging a final volley of shots, the James boys disappeared into the wilds and weren't heard from again for three years.

Less fortunate were the Younger brothers and their single ally, Pitts. Reduced to robbing henhouses to get food, they were hunted like animals until finally trapped in a wooded area near Madelia, some 150 miles from Northfield. Pitts was soon killed, all three of the brothers wounded once more, and still the battle raged. It ended with only Bob Younger on his feet, his gun empty and his right arm broken and useless. Cole had eleven wounds, and Jim was barely alive with wounds in his body and face. Thirteen years later Bob died in prison. Cole and Jim, serving life sentences, eventually were paroled. Jim promptly shot himself, allegedly because a young lady he met didn't

The robber band, killed and/or captured.

Right, a reward poster of the period. *Below*, the Minnesota posse (as photographed in 1876): *from left, top row,* Captain W. W. Murphy, Ben M. Rice, C. A. Pomeroy; *bottom row,* Sheriff James Glispin, G. A. Bradford, Colonel T. L. Vought.

REWARD!
- DEAD OR ALIVE -

$5,000.00 will be paid for the capture of the men who robbed the bank at

NORTHFIELD, MINN.

They are believed to be Jesse James and his Band, or the Youngers.

All officers are warned to use precaution in making arrest. These are the most desperate men in America.

Take no chances! Shoot to kill!!

J. H. McDonald.

The reward notice that spells doom for Jesse James. McDade Collection

return his affection. Cole repented, became a preacher, and devoted himself to saving others by citing his own "misspent" life. He died peacefully in 1916, prepared, he said, to meet his maker.

The James boys, meantime, went traveling. They were reported in California, Tennessee, and Mexico. Three years passed and with the heat off they returned at last to familiar territory. On October 7, 1879, with a reconstituted gang, they robbed a train at Glendale, Missouri—the robbery that was soon to be celebrated in the famous ballad. It was a good haul —some $35,000 in loot.

Love took a hand. Dick Liddell, a junior member of the gang, was quite a swinger for that day and age. He became interested in a blooming young widow who lived on a farm in Ray County, Missouri. Martha returned the interest with interest, and Liddell persuaded Jesse that her farm would make a good hideout. Living there also were Martha's brothers, Charles and Robert Ford, but they seemed to be easygoing, cooperative boys who posed no problems.

Following the next train robbery, the heat went back on. Jesse had combined business with revenge, killing the conductor in cold blood apparently because he had been aboard the Pinkerton special train on its secret mission to bomb the family home. But the public no longer considered such revenge justified, and Governor Thomas Crittenden officially offered $10,000 reward for either Frank or Jesse and $5,000 for any of the other bandits involved in the latest outrage.

As the pressure increased, trouble developed within the gang. Liddell killed Hite, allegedly in a dispute over Martha. Jesse killed Edward Miller, another gang member, suspecting rightly or wrongly that he was about to betray him. Ironically, Liddell became the Judas, giving as justification his fear that Jesse might attempt to avenge Hite's death. Hite, after all, was a cousin of the James boys. But worse was to come. Bob Ford, brother of Liddell's love, paid a secret visit to Governor Crittenden to receive assurance that Liddell would be pardoned and that the $10,000 reward would be paid for a dead Jesse. Ford, obviously, had no intention of attempting to take the outlaw chief alive. The governor was agreeable.

The morning of April 3, 1882, dawned bright and clear. Jesse and his wife were in residence at a house in Saint Joseph, Missouri. There also, waiting their chance, were the brothers Ford.

Top, Mrs. Ford, mother of Robert and Charlie. *Above*, Charlie Ford. *Right*, Robert Ford, who shot and killed Jesse James. Ford was shot and killed in 1892 by Edward O'Kelley.

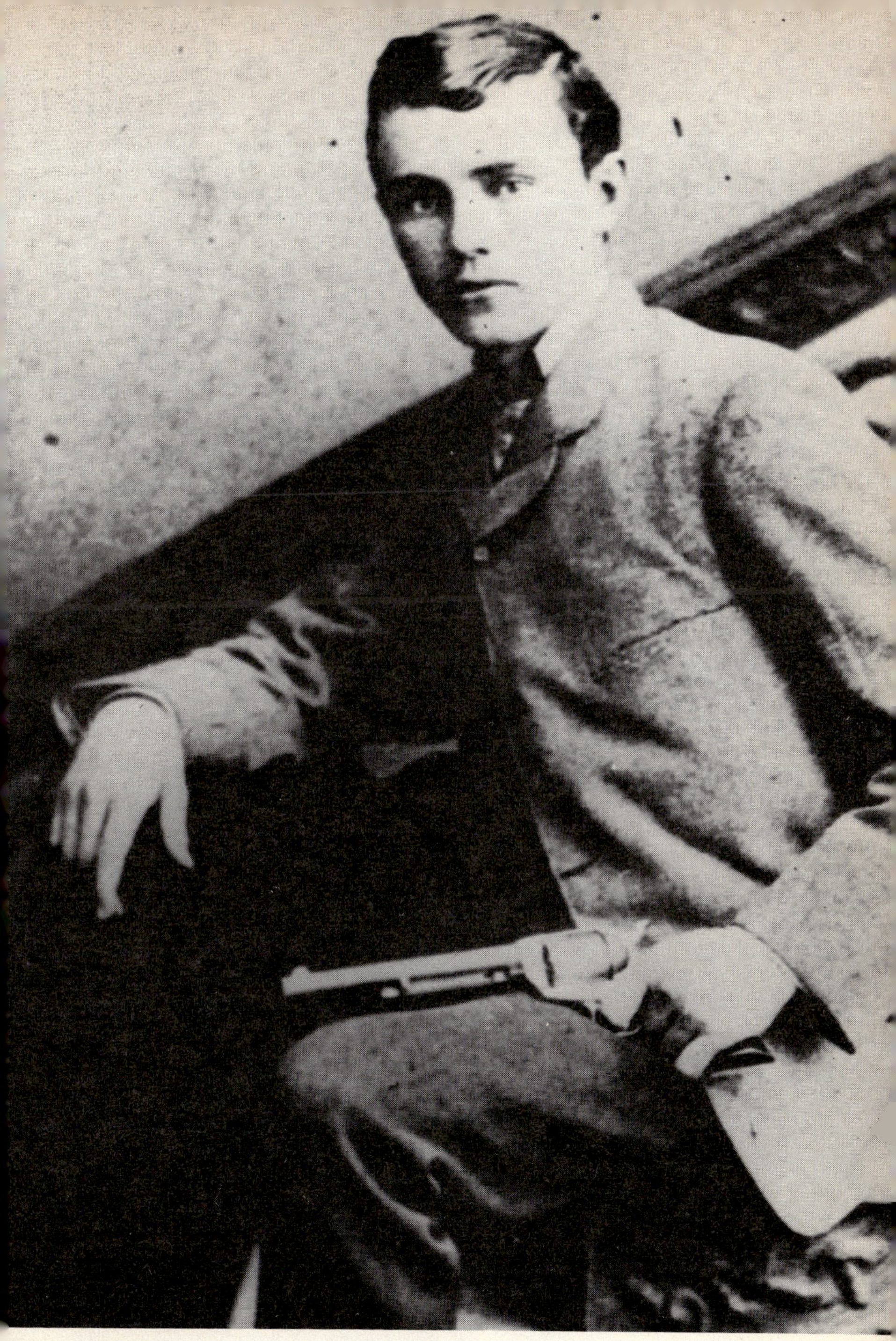

Above, Jesse James's children.
Right, Governor Thomas T. Crittenden.

A contemporary sketch of the shooting of Jesse James.

GOOD BYE, JESSE!

The Notorious Outlaw and Bandit, Jesse James, Killed at St. Joseph

BY R. FORD, OF RAY COUNTY,

A Young Man but Twenty-one Years of Age.

THE DEADLY WEAPON USED

Presented to His Slayer by His Victim but a Short Time Since.

A ROBBERY CONTEMPLATED

Of a Bank at Platte City—To Have Taken Place Last Night.

JESSE IN KANSAS CITY

During the Past Year and Residing on One of the Principal Streets.

KANSAS CITY EXCITED

THE DEAD OUTLAW

Fully Identified by His Mother and Others Who Have Known Him.

RESULT OF THE INQUEST.

Jesse James Came to His Death at the Hands of Robt Ford.

WHAT THE SLAYERS SAY.

Interviews with the Two Fords, Dick Liddil and Gov. Crittenden.

JESSE'S HOME IN THIS CITY.

Interesting Reminiscences of the Bandit and His Family.

THE TRAITOR'S TRIUM

A Day of Excitement and Turmoil

Is Joseph. Is it Jesse? The Question on Every Tongue.

Continuation of the Coroner's Inquest — Dramatic Scenes at Dick Little's Appearance.

Wm. Samuels and Mrs. James Break in Fierce Invectives—Gossip Around the City.

A Talk With Little—Cole Younger Interviewed—Governor Crittenden's Expressed Satisfaction.

Identification of the Remains—The Burial Kearney To-Day—The Trials at Independence.

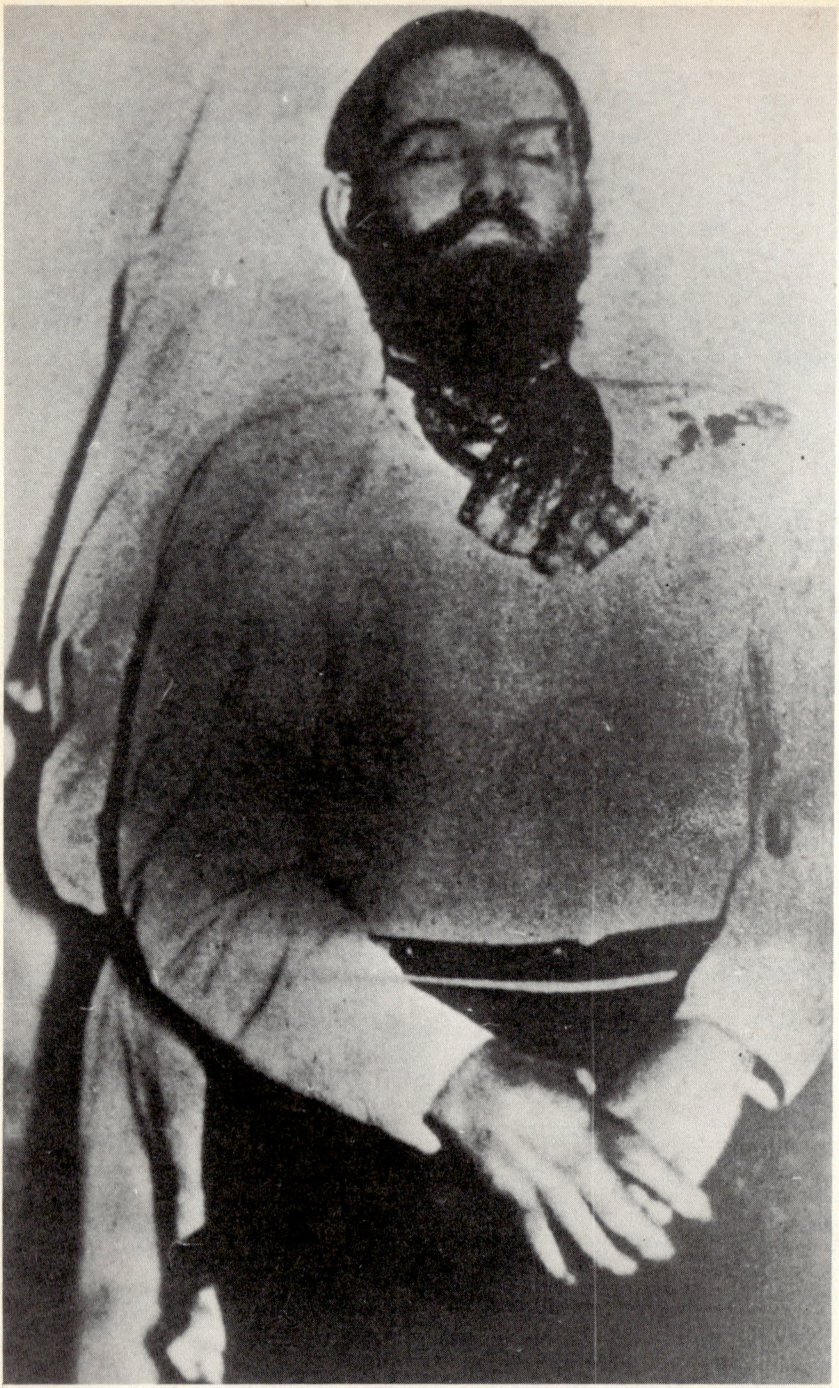

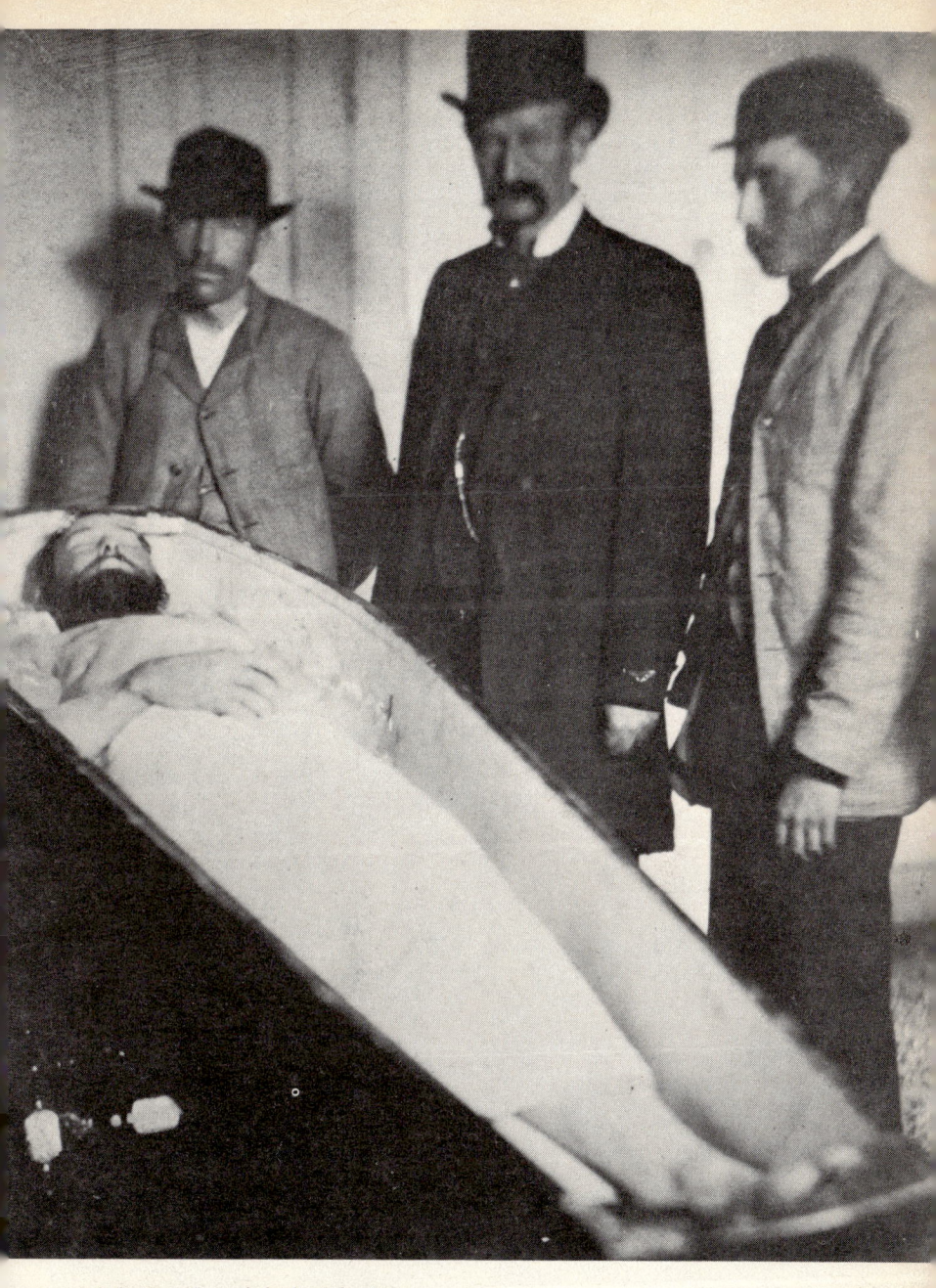

Left, Jesse James's body at the time of the inquest. *Above*, Jesse James in his coffin. Frank, his brother, is in the center. Note that the body is unclothed.

COLE AND JAMES YOUNGER PARDONED
AFTER SERVING TWENTY-FIVE YEARS

St. Paul, Minn., July 10.—The state pardon board today approved the parole of Cole and James Younger, who have been in the Stillwater penitentiary for the past twenty-five years for complicity in the robbery and murder at the time of the raid on the Northfield, Minn., bank.

The Northfield, Minn., bank robbery occurred in the summer of 1876. Six men rode furiously down the main street of the town firing at every one and clearing the streets. They stopped at the bank and while three stood guard on the outside

at him with a knife and in the melee that followed Hayward secured his revolver from a drawer and several shots were exchanged. Citizens began to open fire on the outside, and fearing to remain longer

the bandits fled from the town. The gang was afterwards found to consist of the two James boys, the three Youngers, Cole, Jim and Bob, and Charlie Pitts. It was fourteen days after the robbery

ROBERT YOUNGER
THREE YEARS
BEFORE HIS DEATH

COLEMAN YOUNGER
AS HE IS
TODAY

JAMES YOUNGER
AS HE WAS
15 YEARS AGO

COLEMAN YOUNGER
15 YEARS AGO

JAMES YOUNGER
AS HE IS
TODAY

HENRY WHEELER

Bob Younger, Fr... ...red. Two cle... ...receiving a b... ...f. Cashier J... ... open the ... ... James

when the Younger boys were captured and Charlie Pitts was killed. The two James boys escaped entirely. Bob Younger was so seriously injured in the fight in the bank that his companions were forced to abandon their horses and take to the woods. It is said the James boys finally refused to allow the wounded man to hinder their progress, and left the others. Cole and Jim were both wounded but they stuck to Bob. Day after day they dragged out their painful, halting flight, mostly at night.

Jesse decided to take a walk in the yard. He removed his coat, leaving his two guns visible. Apparently fearing someone might notice and become suspicious, he unstrapped his gunbelt and placed the rig on the bed with his coat. Starting to the door, he stopped suddenly, picked up a cloth, and climbed up on a chair. Apparently he planned to dust a picture hanging on the wall. It was the opportunity the Fords had been seeking for weeks. They drew their guns. Although Jesse's back was turned, he either saw or heard something. His head started to turn but in that instant Bob Ford fired. The range was about four feet. The bullet entered the base of the skull and exited over the left eye. Jesse fell backward to the floor. Bob Ford told a coroner's inquest:

"After the shooting, I told Mrs. James it was accidental, but she would not believe me. I went directly from Jesse's house to the telegraph station and sent a dispatch to Governor Crittenden, informing him of what I had done."

The Fords collected their blood money. Four years later Charley Ford killed himself. Ten years after Jesse's death, Bob Ford—now infamous as "that dirty little coward"—was killed in a fight over a woman.

Jesse's legend was secure. The fact that he had been shot in the back with his guns out of reach supplied the needed element of tragedy to round out his melodramatic career. Frank, left leaderless, decided to surrender. His wife and one-armed mother, fearing he would be gunned down for the reward, made the arrangements; and the outlaw turned himself in to none other than the governor of Missouri. The requirements of law made a trial necessary; the requirements of public sentiment made an acquittal inevitable. The state saw no point in pushing additional charges and Frank went free. He died in 1915 with his boots off, but there were holes in his socks.

In the byways of America they still sing of Jesse.

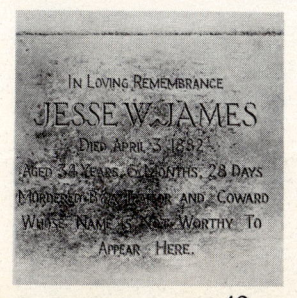

Opposite page, the newspaper report of the Younger brothers' pardon. *Left,* Jesse James's tombstone after the body was reburied. The first stone had been chipped away by the inevitable souvenir hunters.

Belle Starr, well equipped to defend herself, or to rob others.

2
Go Home and Die

SOMEONE SOMEDAY MAY attempt to prove the existence of a WASP Mafia in the Wild, Wild West and blame much of the lawless activity from the end of the Civil War to the beginning of the twentieth century on bad genes owned in common by three outlaw families.

The theory will be based largely on blood relationships said to exist between first, the James and Younger families, and second, between the Youngers and the Daltons.

A key to the Younger-Dalton kinship would be Belle Starr, known to dime novels and Hollywood as a "bandit queen." It seems that after helping Jesse James pull that very first bank robbery at Liberty, Missouri, Cole Younger rode south to Texas and seduced Myra Belle Shirley, a dark-haired beauty just turned eighteen. Leaving her pregnant, he headed on down the trail.

Myra named her daughter Pearl Younger, and she grew up to be a pretty young thing. Meanwhile, Myra became Belle Starr, the happy hooker of the Middle Border. With the single exception of Cole, all her men came to violent ends—and she had a lot of them. Some, like her Indian husband, Sam Starr, were murdered, some were hanged, and some died in action against the forces of law and order.

Meanwhile, her daughter reached marrying age. And our Mafia expert of the future might now note that the mother of of the Dalton boys was a Younger before her marriage to Lewis Dalton. Was it Pearl, the daughter of Belle?

Alas, the wife of Dalton was Adeline, a respectable teenager from Independence, Missouri. Most of her children turned out to be respectable too, but when you have fifteen there's always room for a rotten apple or two in the barrel.

Top left, Belle Starr at the age of sixteen. *Top right*, Cole Younger. *Below*, Pearl Starr, Belle's daughter.

REWARD
$10,000
IN GOLD COIN
Will be paid by the U. S. Government for the apprehension
DEAD OR ALIVE
of
SAM and BELLE STARR
Wanted for Robbery, Murder, Treason and other acts against the peace and dignity of the U. S.

THOMAS CRAIL
Major, 8th Missouri Cavalry, Commanding

A reward poster of the period. *Below,* Belle's cabin, a famous hangout for outlaws. When a posse appeared to be on the way, she hid her friends in a mountain cave nearby.

Pearl Younger ended as a madam in Fort Smith. If she gave birth to any outlaws their names have been lost to history. But our Mafia expert need not despair. Pearl may not figure in this "family" history, but even Cole Younger agreed he was related to Adeline Dalton. She wasn't his aunt, he insisted, but a cousin three or four times removed.

So there it is. If someone wants to blame Younger blood for the Daltons' career they may do so and, at the same time, relate the Youngers to the Jameses. Such a thesis would make as much sense as some popular theories about the Mafia, but the objective observer could shoot it as full of holes as Cole after Northfield. Realistically, there was nothing connecting the three families in the wilds of the West to compare with Mafia members living in an Italian ghetto where blood lines resembled a plate of spaghetti. It is far safer to insist that the Dalton boys admired the Jameses and Youngers for the same reasons youths today seek to emulate Henry Aaron or Joe Willie Namath. Modern sports are a little less violent perhaps.

The first five sons born to Lewis and Adeline turned out to be good men. And that was lucky since their father tended to wander off as soon as his wife became pregnant, leaving his family to find food where it could. The older boys assumed the burden as they grew into it; with pressure eased, the next five felt free to go to the devil.

Grattan, known as Grat, was the oldest of wild Daltons and something of a bully. Bill, two years younger, was the con-man of the family. Frank was a regular guy, famous only for his ability to cuss. Bob was credited with brains as well as courage. Emmett, the youngest of the team, worshipped Bob but resembled Bill in his ability to confuse the issue.

Growing up in Cass County, Missouri, the boys enjoyed being pointed out to visitors as cousins of Cole Younger. Eventually they acquired a horse which allegedly had belonged to Jesse James. Their father, seeking to boost his own ego, boasted that he was a personal friend of James and Younger. Logically then, the boys came to manhood wanting to imitate their heroes. It was when their ambition soared and they sought to outstrip Jesse that disaster befell at Coffeyville.

Coffeyville, Kansas, three miles across the line from Indian Territory that later would become Oklahoma, was a tough place in its day. Billy the Kid, while still a kid, lived there. It served as a model for the town of Osage in Edna Ferber's

Above, Belle Starr, ready to ride the outlaw trail. *Right*, her tombstone.

Bob Dalton, in a picture taken in 1889, two years before his death, with his sweetheart Eugenia Moore.

classic novel, *Cimarron*, but its place in history became fixed in 1882—the year Jesse James died—when Lewis Dalton took his family there to live. The ground around Coffeyville was full of oil that sometimes appeared as a gray slime in springs and wells, but of this the Daltons knew nothing. Reality for them was fast horses and a straight-shooting six-gun. They learned to ride and shoot and brag with the best of them and, eventually, Grat and Frank found jobs policing the Cherokee Nation, those dispossessed wanderers from the Great Smoky Mountains of North Carolina. Frank apparently wanted to be an honest lawman. For his pains he was shot down in a fight with a gang smuggling liquor to the Indians. Far from being inspired to avenge their brother, the remaining "wild" Daltons took advantage of the opening Frank's death provided. Grat got Frank's old job and deputized Bob and Emmett to help. They developed a technique of planting illegal liquor in covered wagons approaching town, "discovering" the liquor, and fining the helpless pioneers on the spot. Bill wasn't available, having gone west to find gold and, instead, acquiring a wife. He had gone into politics and had ambitions to be governor—if only he could get over wanting to be Jesse James.

Back home, the brothers three soon lost their badges when their reputations became too smelly to stand. Undisturbed, they turned to horse stealing and so enraged the Cherokees that they sent a small army into Kansas in pursuit. Grat was captured but, apparently, white folks saved his neck. After a few weeks in jail he was freed. He headed for the hills where Bob and Emmett were waiting. Bob, now the unquestioned boss, sent Grat out to visit brother Bill, and proceeded with recruiting three gunslingers to form the Dalton Gang. Joining up were Bitter Creek Newcomb, Bill McElhanie, and Blackface Charley Bryant. Feeling the home country was too hot, the boys rode out to New Mexico Territory and there knocked off a Mexican gambling joint. The Mexicans responded as violently as had the Indians. Quite a pitched battle resulted. Emmett was wounded before the posse gave up the chase. The gang decided to split up for the time being, with Bob and McElhanie going west to join Grat and Bill Dalton. Maybe they could help Bill win election to the legislature. Or maybe he could help them rob a train.

The best evidence indicates that neither happened. Bill and Grat *were* charged with robbing a Southern Pacific train and Grat was convicted. While they were in jail, however, another

Above, John Sontag. *Top right,* George Sontag. *Bottom right,* Chris Evans. *Opposite page,* a reward notice of the period.

CHRIS EVANS—JOHN SONTAG.

$10,000 REWARD—Will be paid for the arrest and delivery to the Sheriff of Fresno county, Cal., or to the Sheriff of Tulare county, Cal., John Sontag and Chris Evans, or $5,000 for the arrest and delivery of either Sontag or Evans, they are wanted for train robberies and the reward is offered jointly by the Southern Pacific and Wells, Fargo & Co., and will be paid upon the arrest and delivery to either of the above sheriffs.

Chris Evans is about 45 years old; a native of Ottawa, Canada; weight about 160 pounds; height 5 feet 3 inches; hair light or sandy; beard sandy and rather dark; eyes blue; when talking grins and smiles; moves his head sideways from shoulder; walks rather fast with springs in both knees; large bony hands; slouching appearance; when talking has a slight Irish accent and blinks his left eye; has a shrill squeaking voice.

John Sontag, alias John Contant, is a native of Manterio, Minn., he is 23 years old; height 5 feet 11 inches; weight 160 pounds; hair dark; medium dark mustache; prominent cheek bones; even cut features; even cut features; complexion fair and rather good looking; lame in right ankle; when he was last seen at Supervisor Ellis' home in company with Chris Evans twenty miles north of Visalia on Sunday Sept. 4th; he wore a dark felt hat; dark pants and vest with coat lighter in color; gold watch and chain. They were both heavily armed and will resist arrest. Address all information to the Sheriff of

Fresno Co., Cal., or Sheriff of Tulare Co., Cal., whom will pay the above reward when delivered to them.

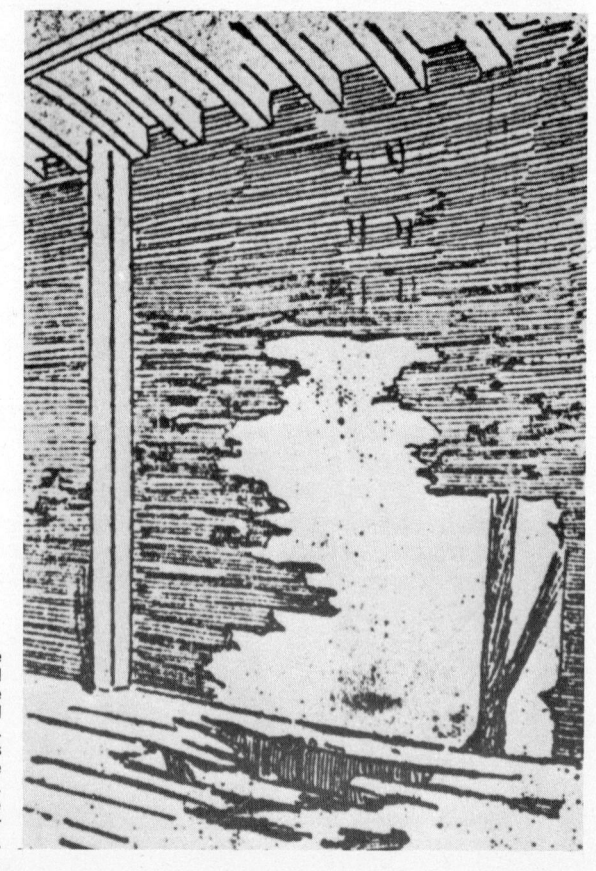

Top, the shattered doorsill of the wrecked express car. The bomb was placed where the X appears. *Right*, the shattered car and flooring.

A WANTON BUTCHERY

Evans and Sontag Attack a Pursuing Posse in the Mountains and Kill Three Men.

They Open Fire on the Officers and Complete Their Work before a Shot

THE MORNING CALL, SAN

THEIR THIRST FOR BLOOD.

Evans and Sontag Said to Have Claimed Yet Another Victim.

EXAMINER, SAN FR.
SATURDAY MOR
AUGUST 6, 1892

BANDITS AT BAY.

The Collis Train Robbers, Tracked to Visalia, Turn Upon the Detectives and Shoot Them.

After Seriously Wounding One Officer and Driving the Other Off They Make

TUESDAY MORNING

SEPTEMBER 14, 1892

EVANS WOUNDED.

Frank Burke Arrives at Visalia With the Bodies of Two Victims.

[Special to the EXAMINER.]

VISALIA, September 13.—Visalia was startled to-day by the report that Evans and Sontag, the Collis train robbers, had killed three of the pursuing party from here, near Sampson's Flat, their favorite rendezvous.

The posse that started out this afternoon returned to town to-night, having met Smith and Burke with the dead bodies of McGinnis and Wilson.

Witty was only slightly wounded.

Burke says he is satisfied he shot and wounded Evans and that the capture of the desperadoes by the parties now in the mountains is only a matter of a short time.

The man Olsen, who was killed, was a mountaineer, and his remains were left in the hills.

John Sontag, wounded and loaded with lead from the guns of a posse. *Left,* news accounts of the period.

train was robbed and suspicion settled on Chris Evans and John Sontag. Both men were bitter foes of the politically active railroad and were fighting a war. The episode involving the Daltons ended when Grat was allowed to escape. He headed home, more than a little disillusioned. In blaming the Daltons so hastily the railroad was not acting on impulse. Bill Dalton was allied with political forces opposed to the railroad, and in accusing him of train robbery, rightly or wrongly, the Southern Pacific destroyed his political career. The same sort of ruthless reaction was employed against the real robbers. Sontag and Evans were just as determined and their struggle took on epic proportions. Wounded and alone, they held out for months against the forces of an economic empire. Sontag died at last with a record amount of lead in his body. Evans lost an eye and an arm but lived to serve time and go free at last. The drama so captured public attention that it was made into a stage play with Eva Evans, daughter of the bandit, playing a star role. She did the railroad more harm public-relations-wise than her father or the Daltons ever did with their guns.

Meanwhile, Bill accepted reality and followed Grat back to Oklahoma. Political ambition wasn't dead, however. He believed he could start again back home where the folks understood that not all Daltons were bad. As he saw it, a respectable Dalton engaged in business and politics could be of great value to the outlaws; and the outlaws, if kept at a proper distance, could be of great value to him. For one thing they might be persuaded to invest some of their loot in the land business that Bill planned to start. Might as well put it into land deals instead of burying it in caves. Once he was established, he assured his wife, he would send for her and the children.

Had the Daltons pulled all the holdups credited to them in the new few years they would have had ample money to invest in land deals. Much as would happen to John Dillinger, they were blamed for every robbery from Kentucky to Kansas, from Minnesota to Mississippi. Bob, the leader, gloried in the notoriety and began to plan his jobs with an eye to their publicity value rather than the loot potential. Ambition stirred and grew strong to surpass Jesse James by robbing two banks at the same time in broad daylight. And, it so happened, he knew where to find two convenient banks. In Coffeyville, Kansas, his old hometown. There he would be performing before neighbors who may not have appreciated his family in the past but would

Some of the Daltons: *top left*, Grat; *right*, Ben, who was not an outlaw. *Bottom left*, Bob; *right*, Emmett.

surely sit up and take notice when their banks were robbed. It was all rather juvenile, perhaps, but it became an obsession. Finally he decided to do it, and, if the take was big enough, to retire to a ranch in Mexico.

On October 1, 1892, Federal Marshal Chris Madsen received some hard intelligence from federal officials in Fort Smith, Arkansas. According to an informer, the Daltons were preparing to rob a bank—either at Van Buren, Arkansas, or Coffeyville, Kansas. Madsen at first thought they would be "damned fools" to hit Coffeyville, but he changed his mind upon learning that Bob had paid a secret visit to the old hometown a few days earlier. A supply of rifles was shipped to Coffeyville and the alarm passed. Apparently without exception the townsmen decided to have a warm welcome waiting for the expatriates.

The gang rode to Coffeyville by easy stages and were poised and ready outside of town as the sun rose on October 5. In the party were Bob, Grat, and Emmett Dalton, Dick Broadwell, and Bill Powers. All five washed and shaved themselves carefully. Obviously, the Daltons wanted to look good as they made history. Their route into town took them past the old farmhouse where the Daltons had lived as teen-agers and scrambled for a living while their father roamed. A glimpse of the past, it could not fail to strengthen their resolve for the future. After this double caper, the Daltons had agreed, they would take their girls and head for Mexico, there to become respectable ranchers. Already the girls were waiting.

Storekeeper Alexander McKenna gave the alarm as the robbers walked into the public square on which the two banks fronted. Their horses they hitched in a back lot connected to the square by an alley.

"There go the Daltons," shouted McKenna, and the warning ran like wildfire down the street.

Bob and Emmett entered the First National. Grat led the way into the Condon Bank. Everything was going according to plan —the Dalton's plan *and* the townspeople's plan.

All went smoothly at the First National—at first. Bob and Emmett collected all the loose cash and cleaned out the vault. Some $21,000 was dumped in a grain sack—shades of Jesse James. The brothers tried to go out the front door using tellers and bank customers as a human shield. A volley from waiting marksmen changed their minds, however, and they went out the back door into an alley. Only one man blocked their path

The Condon Bank, Coffeyville, Kansas.

John J. Kloehr, who fought the Dalton gang in the alley with a shotgun.

and he was gunned down by Bob Dalton, dying three hours later. But there was still several hundred yards to go to reach the alley where the horses were hitched. To get there it was necessary to return to the square. It was as if having escaped from a burning building into a blind alley, they had to return through the building in order to get safely away.

In an exchange of shots, the two Daltons killed two more men. That got them free again, but, spotting Tom Ayres with a rifle in his hand, Bob couldn't resist. Ayres was a cashier in the just-robbed bank. Obviously he hadn't been intimidated. So Dalton lifted his Winchester and burned him down from seventy-five yards away. The bullet hit just below the left eye. Ayres lived.

Satisfied, the brothers ran to the alley and dashed down it to their horses. But where was Grat Dalton and his two companions? Back in the Condon Bank apparently. Bob and Emmett looked at each other a long moment. In their hands was a bag of cash, their best haul yet. Within minutes they could be out of danger and on their way to Mexico and a new life. Instead, they turned back up the alley to help their brother. After all, Frank James had come back through a hail of lead to rescue Jesse at Gallatin.

Grat, following orders, had no problem at the Condon Bank until reaching the inner safe of the vault. The door was closed. When he ordered a cashier to open it he was given the oldest excuse in the business—the door was set on a time lock and would not open until the appointed hour. Actually, the appointed hour had already passed, but Grat didn't bother to check the handle. He decided to wait.

Writers, who disagree about nineteenth-century bandits as readily as about twentieth-century Mafia punks, vary as to how long the wait lasted. But, whatever its duration, it was fatal. Townsmen who had spotted Bob and Emmett in the First National soon discovered that mischief was afoot in the other bank as well. And they prepared. Five, or fifteen, minutes later, Grat, carrying the loot, went out the front door. He got about twenty feet before the first bullet hit him. He dropped the bag of money and staggered on as more bullets plowed into his huge frame. Somehow he reached the alley where the horses waited and, falling, found cover. There Bob and Emmett reached him.

Grat's companions were also having problems. Broadwell

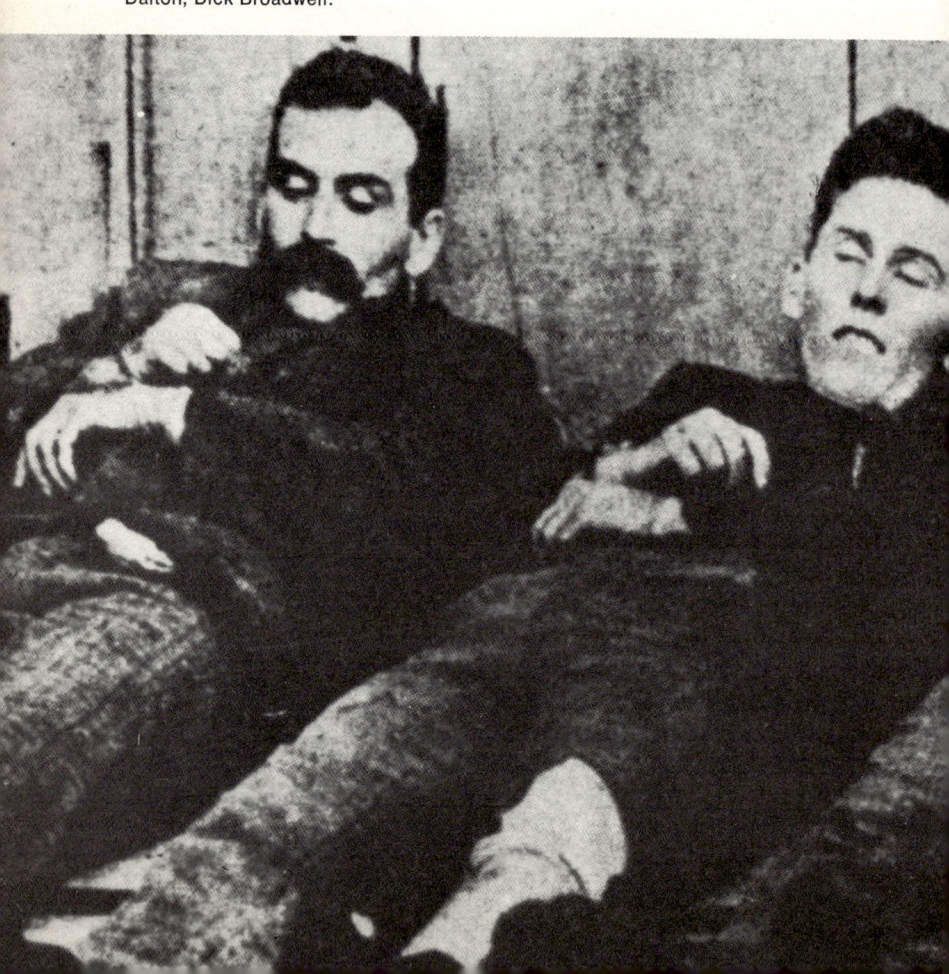

The bodies, some handcuffed: *from left*, Bill Powers, Bob Dalton, Grat Dalton, Dick Broadwell.

DALTONS!

The Robber Gang Meet Their Waterloo in Coffeyville.

LITERALLY WIPED OUT

SHOT THE DALTONS.

Four of the Gang Killed in a Fight in Coffeyville, Kas.

FOUR CITIZENS ARE DEAD

The Desperadoes Made an Attempt to Loot Two Banks.

TERRIBLE FIGHT RESULTS.

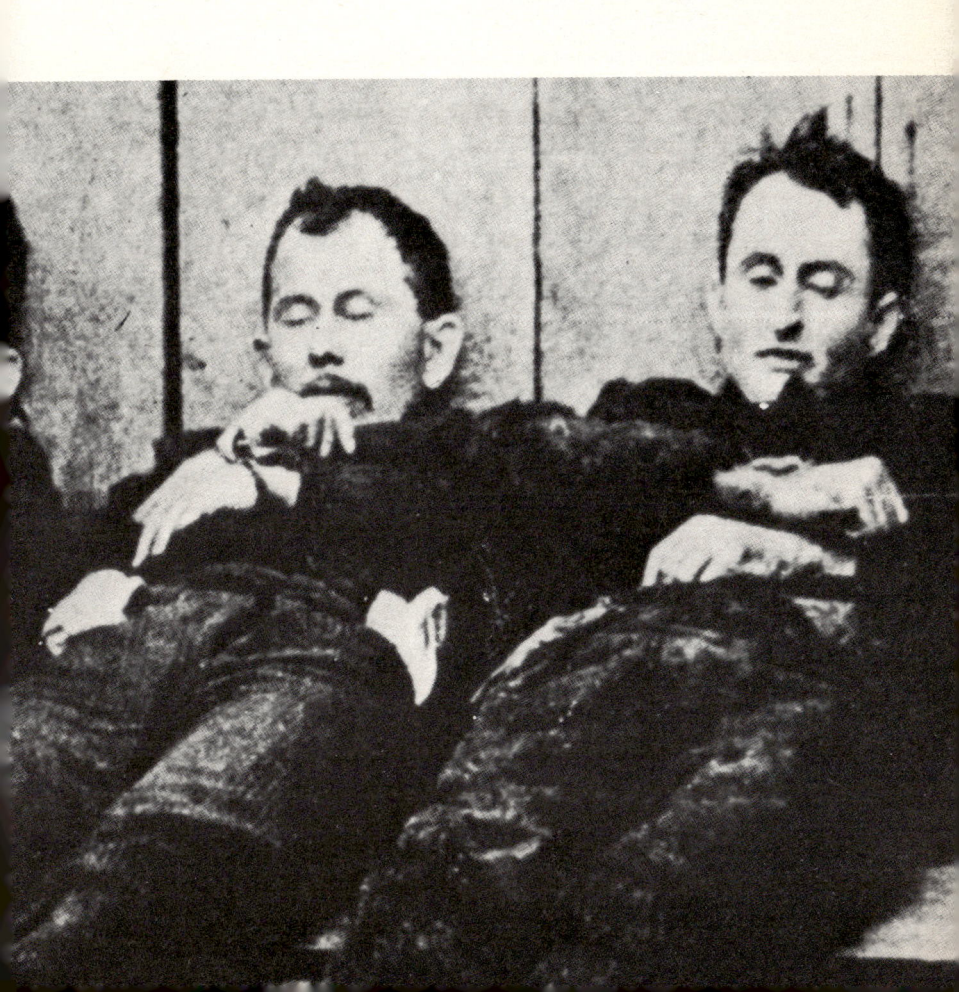

was hit in the back as he sprinted across the square, but found cover under a pile of lumber. Bill Powers was also wounded, but managed to find shelter. The firing died as the townspeople regrouped and sought new positions.

City Marshal Charles Connelly, noted for his silky beard, cut across a vacant lot toward the alley where the horses stood. Grat, bleeding and near death, spotted him and fired almost instinctively. Connelly fell mortally wounded. A moment later it was a score for the other side as Powers reached the horses and was shot down as he tried to mount. Broadwell actually climbed into the saddle and galloped out of town before falling out of the saddle dead a half-mile beyond the city limits. The three Daltons were left to fight alone.

Bob was next to go. One bullet wounded him and he staggered into the sights of John Kloehr who put a slug into his chest, killing him.

Grat, still alive, staggered toward the horses. Kloehr, reputed to be the best shot in town, made it two in a row with a bullet into Grat's neck.

Only Emmett was left. Picking up the sack of loot from Bob's dead hand, he ducked down the alley to the horses. Somehow, he reached them and climbed aboard. As the citizens began running for mounts to give chase, Emmett paused, turned, rode back to his fallen brother, leaned down to lift the inert body, and fell as a double-barreled shotgun sent two loads of buckshot into his back.

The score: four of five bandits dead, one wounded; four citizens dead, three wounded; four horses dead.

Emergency surgery saved Emmett's life, despite the intrusion of a lynch mob in the middle of the operation. The surgeon assured the sensation seekers his patient was going to die anyway. So the boys went over to the jail where some enterprising fellow had discovered that by pumping Grat's arm blood could be forced out of the hole in his throat. Way out, man!

When he learned he would live, Emmett began enjoying his fame. Like Jesse James he had achieved immortality of a sort. After a fifteen-year stretch in the penitentiary, he betook himself to Hollywood where he had the pleasure of seeeing his bad book, *When the Daltons Rode*, turned into a worse movie. He died there in 1937.

Bill Dalton remained. Upon hearing of the Coffeyville Massacre, he escorted his mother and sister to the town to visit

Emmett and behaved modestly enough. But, inside, he was churning. Any chance for a new beginning in politics was as dead as Bob and Grat. Moreover, he resented being mentioned in footnotes when his stupid brothers were the talk of the territory and of much of the nation. Had he been along, he boasted, the raid wouldn't have been bungled.

Such a mood led him ultimately to Bill Doolin, one of the original sidekicks of the Daltons. For one reason or another, Doolin had not taken part in the Coffeyville venture. Now he was recruiting a new gang, and he accepted Bill as a member. The gang achieved several successes but Doolin soon recognized that the presence of a Dalton was like waving a red flag in the face of a longhorn bull. Every lawman in the West wanted to get the last bandit of that name. So Doolin, being a man of some intelligence, paid off Bill and sent him riding a lone trail. Bill, determined now to outdo Jesse James *and* his brothers, went down to Texas and with some new sidekicks knocked off the Longview National Bank, killing three men in the process. They got away with $2,000, but a posse caught up with Bill on June 8, 1894, and surrounded the house in which he was hiding. Bill jumped from a window and ran, but was mowed down by bullets. The wild, wild Daltons had reached the end of the trail at last.

In death they live as legends.

A cartoon of the period—a rare commentary of the day, showing what Coffeyville thought of the Daltons.

* * * * *

Castle Gate, Utah, buried in a gorge of Price River, was a helluva place to pull a train job and some members of the "Train Robbers' Syndicate" opposed it. But Elza Lay, the so-called educated robber, thought it could be done and Butch Cassidy respected Lay's opinion. All it took was some business-like planning and preparation.

Since Butch's release from the Wyoming penitentiary the year before, he had been attempting to convince the residents of Hole-in-the-Wall that crime could be just as much fun and a lot more profitable if intelligence as well as intestinal fortitude was employed. Even the name that he had coined for the gang was part of the educational process, and it is perhaps a measure of his problem that the syndicate should be remembered in history instead as "the Wild Bunch."

The coup at Castle Gate would be a lesson in point, Cassidy decided, and with Lay he studied the situation. The objective would be the Pleasant Valley Coal Company's payroll which came in about noon on the train from Salt Lake City some eighty-five miles away. All the miners would be standing around, of course, and some of them could shoot as well as dig. Unless one took the train, the only way out of town was down the gorge for about four miles where finally the sheer walls of the canyon flattened out a little at Gordon Creek. One would need fast horses for the getaway and then perhaps some relays across the wild country to safety. The big problem was getting the horses into town. Since there was nothing there but the river, the railroad, and the mine, horses were almost non-existent and strangers on horseback would automatically arouse suspicion—especially on payday.

Lay came up with the solution. The robbers—and only two men would be needed—would pose as racehorse owners enroute to Salt Lake City. Horse racing was a popular sport and racing rigs were easily recognized. Moreover, there was something about the sport that made even cynical men relax and become suckers. Still is, for that matter.

With that problem settled, the rest was routine. Sturdy horses bred for endurance could be spotted and reliable men left to guard them at convenient intervals. Someone—Joe Walker got the job—could cut the telegraph wires down river at Price so no alarm could be given quickly. Once ahead of the pursuers it would be just a matter of hard riding.

Butch Cassidy

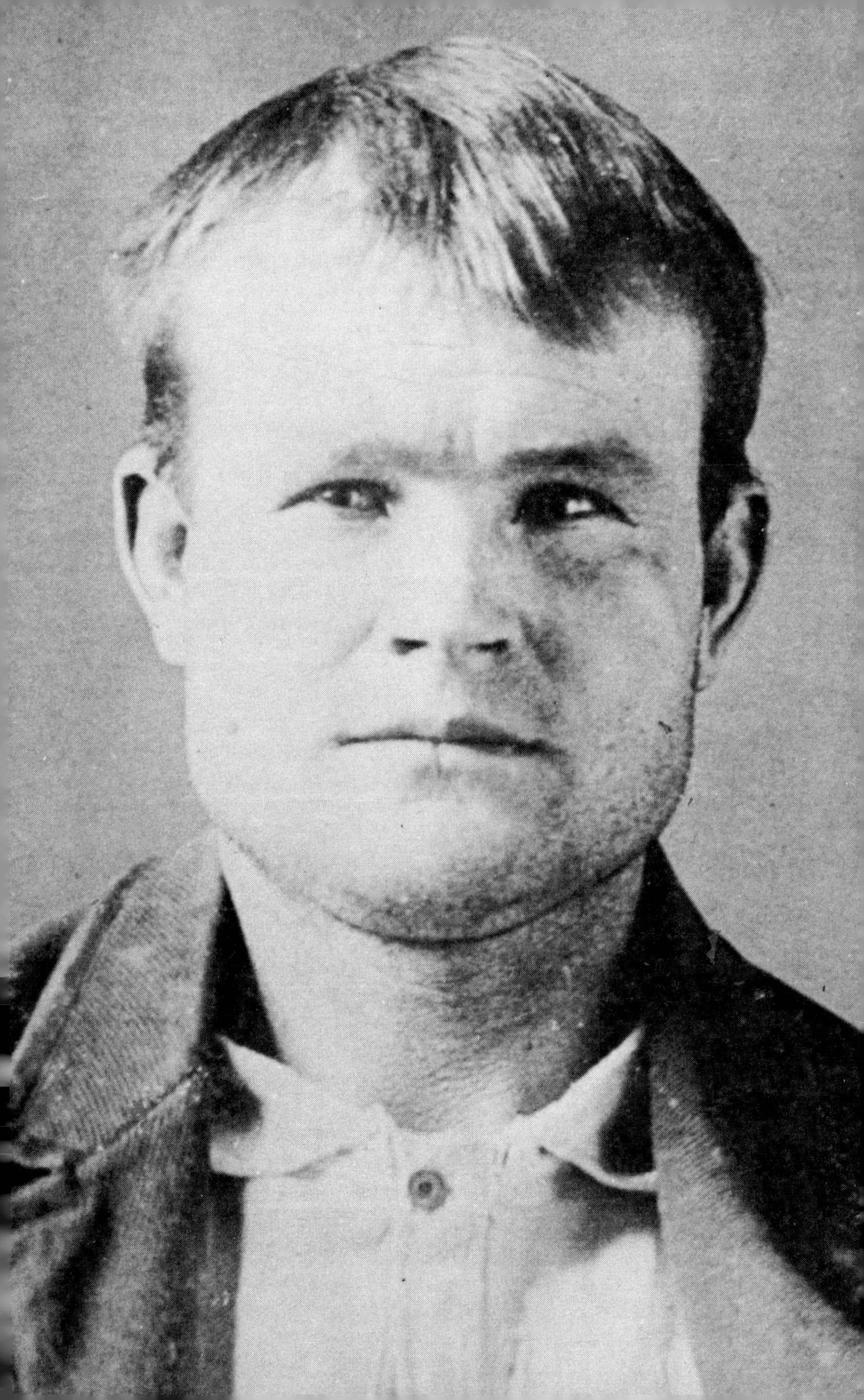

Butch Cassidy country, the area used by the Hole-in-the-Wall Gang as their base of operations in Wyoming.

Butch and Lay enjoyed the planning so much they decided to do the job themselves. Everything worked wonderfully at first. Arriving in town just before noon, Butch got off Babe and handed the reins to Lay who remained astride Kid. Butch strolled over to the stairs leading to the second-floor offices of the coal company and sat down on a box. A miner stopped to admire the horses and talk about racing. No sweat. Up the canyon the train tooted, alerting the paymaster. He had a sore foot and was wearing bedroom slippers—in a town without women there was no need to dress fancy. Downstairs he came, almost stumbling over Butch's outstretched leg. Routine. To the depot he went, returning quickly with a leather satchel and several bags of coins. Butch let him pass again, then got to his feet. As the paymaster stepped on the stairs, he felt a gun in his back. Moving quickly now, Cassidy tossed two of the money sacks to Lay. The unexpected sight of a heavy bag flying close to her nose spooked Babe, Butch's horse. She reared and jerked free as Lay caught the sacks like they were basketballs. Down the street went Babe—in the right direction anyway.

Lay gave chase and Butch, still clutching the satchel of cash, followed on foot. There was no time to gag the paymaster who started yelling at the top of his voice. Being a self-sufficient fellow, however, he didn't wait for help but padded upstairs to his office where a rifle waited. From the window he opened fire.

Lay, utilizing his long experience as a cattle rustler, managed to trap Babe against a railroad trestle. Cassidy, running hard, mounted from the rear, grabbed the reins, and was off. At a section house down the line they paused to put on the saddles they had hidden there and to transfer the loot to special bags they had brought along. As they prepared to remount they heard the train coming.

The paymaster had abandoned his rifle and raced back to the depot only to learn that the telegraph wires had been cut. There was no way to alert the sheriff at Price. Yes, by God, there was! He ran back to the train, ordered the engine cut loose, and climbed into the cab. The engineer was ready to roll and roll they did—passing the outlaws without seeing them—and coming into Price with the whistle screaming. For a man in bedroom shoes, the paymaster was an enterprising individual.

Much good it did him. The robbers turned up Gordon Creek and reached their first relay point on schedule. Changing horses they proceeded at a slower pace. Joe Walker soon caught up with them. They gave him the money and told him to split. Now, if they were captured there would be no hard evidence to convict. At Mexican Bend they found fresh horses and a small black dog. The pup, named Sunday, took a shine to Butch and followed as Cassidy and Lay rode on.

Meanwhile, from Price, the message had gone out. Posses rode from several directions. The paymaster, still in his bedroom shoes, led one. Two groups mistook each other for the bandits at one point and fought a pitched battle. That discouraged most of them, but a few brave souls took up the pursuit and soon overtook Sunday who was getting a bit footsore. Up ahead, Butch spotted the law on his tail but he was more concerned about the faithful dog he could see in the distance. At his orders, Lay stopped on a ridge and started shooting at the posse while Butch rode around behind the good guys and rescued the dog. The shots, meanwhile, had completely confused the pursuers who dug in for a batttle. By the time they discovered their mistake the bandits were so far ahead as to make chase useless.

Clutching the dog, Butch rejoined his men convinced that he had demonstrated that business and pleasure did mix if one used his head. The $8,000 taken in the robbery was additional proof, but Sunday was the best evidence.

Elza Lay, right-hand man of Butch Cassidy, who died peacefully in 1934.

Above left, Bill McCarty; *right*, Tom McCarty. *Below*, the Parker homestead in Circleville, Utah.

Left to right: standing, William Carver, Harvey Logan (Kid Curry); *sitting,* Harry Longbaugh (The Sundance Kid), Ben Kilpatrick (The Tall Texan), Robert Leroy Parker (Butch Cassidy).

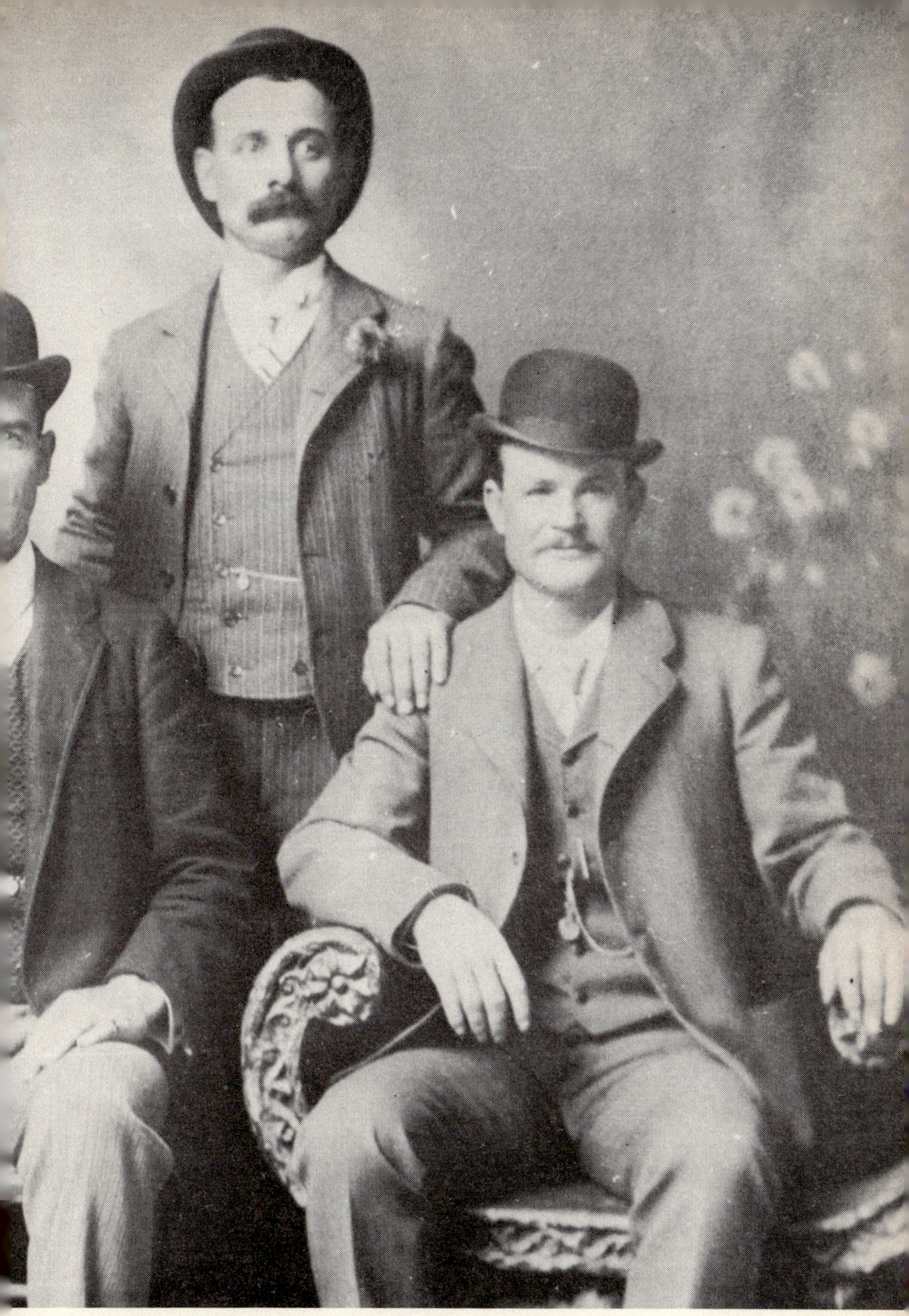

Butch by any standard was a remarkable man, but when measured against most western outlaws he comes out ten feet tall. Born in Circle Valley, Utah, on April 13, 1866, his name was Robert LeRoy Parker. To protect his respectable Mormon parents he adopted the name of a man he admired, tough Mike Cassidy. "Butch" was a nickname earned while working briefly as a butcher. Ironically, Elza Lay adopted the name McGuiness after a friend of his youth, but he later fell in love with a strong-minded young lady who made him marry her under his real name. Butch could understand that, but no woman ever required such a legalization of relations from him.

Upon leaving home, Cassidy learned the art of cattle rustling and became acquainted with the vast wilderness area of Utah, Wyoming, Colorado, and Arizona. There were mountain hideouts so isolated and protected by natural barriers that no lawman dared venture near. Robber's Roost and Hole-in-the-Wall became famous in history and in fiction. In the process of learning his trade, the handsome Butch served an apprenticeship with the McCarty Gang. Their biggest coup was the First National Bank of Denver on March 30, 1889. Butch waved a bottle of water under the nose of the bank's president and told him it was nitroglycerin—a technique widely used by bankrobbers and skyjackers ninety years later. The loot was $21,000 which, Butch agreed, was not bad for two men. Later that same year, they hit another bank in Telluride, Colorado. Closely pursued, they headed out of town. One of the pursuers, whose name has been overlooked by kindly historians, was better mounted than the rest and suddenly found that he and he alone was about to catch up with the bandits. What to do? Well, there was always one excuse for any occasion. He slowed down and stopped to "answer a call of nature." Butch, who regretfully was about to shoot him, holstered his gun and rode on laughing so hard he almost fell from the saddle. After that, the money they had stolen seemed like a bonus.

But life wasn't always so funny. The McCartys decided to move to Oregon. Butch stayed behind and drifted. One day a roaming posse came across a cabin he shared with another rider. Deciding the men were cattle rustlers—which they were —the posse tried to take them. Butch fought bravely, suffering a scalp wound and a broken jaw, but eventually he was captured.

Convicted of rustling, Butch was paroled after eighteen

Annie Rogers and Harvey Logan (Kid Curry).

SAINT PAUL PIONEER PRESS
TUESDAY, JULY 12, 1904.

KID CURRY IN HIS GRAVE

Photographs Reveal That Notorious "Bad Man" Killed Himself While Chased After Committing Train Robbery.

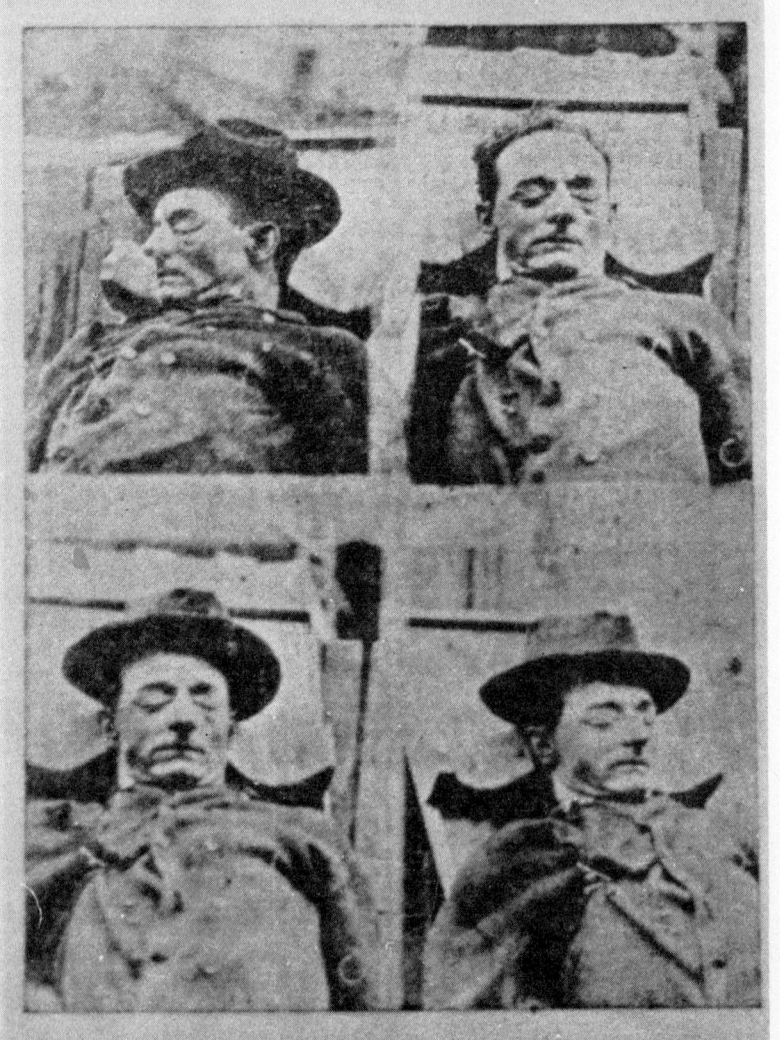

BANDIT "KID CURRY."

months on condition he raise no hell in Wyoming. He was agreeable, having had the leisure to do some thinking. Henceforth trains would be his targets. He would form the Train Robbers' Syndicate, drawing men from the small army of outlaws who hung out at Hole-in-the-Wall.

Despite the object lesson Castle Gate provided, the Syndicate never took itself very seriously. Jobs were pulled at intervals as need or impulse suggested. When you conduct business for fun—and that was Cassidy's goal—the office hours are sure to be flexible. Personnel varied, but Cassidy became close friends with Harry Longbaugh, the kid from Sundance in Crook County, Wyoming; Ben Kilpatrick, famous as the Tall Texan; Elza Lay, who had ridden with him at Castle Gate; and Harvey Logan, the legendary Kid Curry. The latter was a moody man and, unlike most members of the Wild Bunch, a killer by instinct.

From the start, Cassidy planned retirement in South America. Sooner or later, he argued, the homesteaders would spread like ants over the West, bringing with them law and order. Money would be needed to make the transition, but Butch was in no great hurry to accumulate it. Lay disagreed. He too wanted to go south and the quicker the better. When Butch turned down a proposal to hit the Colorado & Southern at Folsom, New Mexico, Lay recruited Kid Curry and Sam Ketchum. Curry was always ready for action and Ketchum was always hungry. But Butch's hunch proved right. The express car was separated from the rest of the train and the safe blown open. Nothing was found. Disgusted, the three robbers rode away. The sheriff at Trinidad, Colorado, was soon hot on their heels with a posse. In the battle that followed, the sheriff and a deputy were killed, four men were wounded. Ketchum and Lay were also wounded, putting the burden of defense on the cold-eyed Kid Curry. Ketchum was left behind, allegedly at his request, and was found next day unconscious on the ground beside his horse. He died of blood poisoning a few days later. Curry got Lay safely to New Mexico and left him in an isolated cabin while he rode to the nearest town for supplies. While he was away, Lay was mistaken for a horse thief by another posse. Assuming, naturally enough, that he was wanted for the train robbery, Lay put up a good fight. When his gun was empty he used his fists, but was soon overcome and eventually identified. Sentenced to life imprisonment, he won the friendship of the warden during a prison riot in 1895. The convicts took the warden's wife and daughters hostage. Lay, who was trusted by both sides, managed to settle the riot and recover the hostages without hurt. As a reward he was pardoned on January 10, 1906. Upon release he went to Wyoming, married the daughter of a leading rancher—who insisted he take back his real name—and moved eventually to Los Angeles where he died peacefully in 1934.

Cassidy, meanwhile, made a proposition to the governor of Utah. In return for amnesty he would retire to South America and dissolve the Train Robbers' Syndicate. There was considerable interest in the idea, but Butch got tired of the long-range discussions and went off to rob a train at Tipton, Wyoming. Apparently he considered his promise to the governor "inoperative." Also along was Laura Bullion, the girl companion of the Tall Texan, and Etta Place, Sundance's mistress.

The loot—and the amount is a matter of some dispute—wasn't sufficient to rate as the final caper, so they decided to do the unexpected and rob a bank. The First National at Winnemucca, Nevada, was selected. Once again, a certain personal touch can be noted. Cassidy and the Sundance Kid decided to do the actual stickup, but Bill Carver—a veteran of the Wild Bunch—was assigned to wander into town alone. Dressed in old clothes and carrying an ancient bedroll, he was to pause as if to rest in the lobby of the bank. In the bedroll, of course, was a concealed rifle, to be used only if needed. The robbery was successful, and the five men—Cassidy, Sundance, Kid Curry, Carver, and the Tall Texan—rode down to Fort Worth, Texas, for a farewell celebration.

Headquarters for the affair was a place known to all of them —and most other outlaws and politicians of the day—as Fannie Porter's Sporting House. It was at Fannie's place that Kid Curry had met his mistress, Annie Rogers, and she was back for the reunion with him. The men posed for a picture, wearing dark suits, derbies, and gold watch fobs across their muscled stomachs. A print of the picture was sent to the First National at Winnemucca, with a note from Butch conveying his thanks. An enlargement hangs in the bank today.

But Kid Curry wasn't ready to retire—to South America or anywhere else. He persuaded Butch that one more job should be attempted. Sundance and Etta went on to New York, and the others headed for Montana. There on July 3, 1901, the

Harry Longbaugh (The Sundance Kid)
and the beautiful Etta Place.

IDENTITY OF TRAIN ROBBERS KNOWN

Detectives Employed by the Railroad Say They Are Old Hands.

OUTLAWS OBTAINED OVER FORTY-ONE THOUSAND.

NEARLY ALL THE PLUNDER WAS IN BANK NOTES AND EASILY DISPOSED OF.

The Gang Now Believed to Be in the Little Rockies, a Wild Section in Montana, Where Pursuit Is Difficult.

THE ROBBERS ARE SURROUNDED

Great Northern Express Thieves Pocketed in the Heart of the Little Rockies and Sheriff's Men Are Gathering.

A DESPERATE BATTLE IS NOW INEVITABLE

The Outlaws Cannot Go Much Further, Owing to the Nature of the Country and the Strength of the Force That Is Gathering to Shut Them Off.

The posse that trailed the Wild Bunch: *from left,* George Hiatt, T. T. Keliher, Joe Lefores, H. Davis, Si Funk, Jeff Carr.

MONTANA OUTLAWS CORNERED

A Sheriff's Posse Said to Have Located the

FEAR ROBBERS HAVE ESCAPED.

Little Hope of Sheriffs Overtaking Men Who Up the Great Northern.

MAY BE HEADED FOR "HOLE IN

Train Robbers' Syndicate was officially liquidated. As the train approached Wagner, Curry stepped into the cab and ordered the engineer to stop over a bridge. While several members of the Wild Bunch, including the women, fired enough shots to discourage the passengers, Curry and Cassidy blew open the safe. The haul was some $41,500. Six months later, after joining Sundance and Etta in New York, Butch deposited his share in a bank in Buenos Aires.

"The Wild West is finished," said Cassidy to Curry.

"Not as long as I'm around," the Kid replied.

Curry believed his own words, and spent the next two years wandering around the country, from Tennessee to California. Captured once, he escaped from jail and kept on wandering. Finally, in 1904, as "Tap Duncan," he assembled a gang of amateurs and robbed a train near Parachute, Colorado. It was a bust, but the posse that followed wasn't composed of amateurs. They trapped the robbers in a canyon. Kid, badly wounded, remained as a rear guard while his comrades made a break for

From the film *Butch Cassidy and the Sundance Kid:* Robert Redford (*left*) as Sundance and Paul Newman as Butch Cassidy.

it. Then, as the sun rose, he shot himself in the head. It was a year later before the body was finally identified as Curry. And some people who knew the Kid well were never convinced.

Much the same verdict must be given for Butch and Sundance. They bought a ranch in Argentina and settled down with Etta Place. But a Pinkerton detective got on their trail and forced them after three years to run for it. Robbing while running just came natural, and the boys began knocking over banks. Eventually Etta became ill, and Sundance brought her back to the states for treatment. But his friendship was greater than his love, and he returned to help his pardner. By now it was obvious that the pursuit would continue as long as they lived. So, perhaps, the wily Cassidy decided that, officially, they had to die.

Allegedly, after robbing a silver-mine payroll from a mule train, Sundance and Butch were trapped by soldiers in a small hut at San Vicente, Bolivia. The soldiers shot the hut full of holes all night long and next morning entered it to find two bodies. Apparently Butch had killed Sundance and then turned his revolver on himself in the Kid Curry tradition.

The story persists, however, that the dead men were not Sundance and Butch, that, somehow, they had pulled a final fast one. Indeed one reputable author with close ties to Butch's folks in Utah insists that Butch visited his family there in 1929. It is possible. Certainly, nothing would have given Butch Cassidy more fun than to attend his own funeral, and Butch was a man who liked his pleasure. Especially when he could combine it with business.

So perhaps in death they lived—and not just in legend.

In this 1930 photo, Eddie Gong, leader of the Hip Sing Tong, inspects his cleavers. The Boo How Doi tong war that had broken out in New York's Chinatown brought new violence after two decades of peace.

3
Blind White Devils

ONE TURNS FROM the wide open spaces with some regret, but balance requires a look at the smelly ghettos where immigrants from Europe and Asia sizzled awhile in the melting pot before adjusting to the American system of free enterprise.

It was in some measure due to the pressure of those "miserable millions" that "old Americans" pushed westward ho in the first place. Moreover, it is important to illustrate once again that crime is not the province of any single ethnic or national group. The blood of non-WASPs was just as red when spilled, and the Italians, the Irish, and, yes, the Chinese, were equally subject to that restlessness which only revenge, glory, or pure love can appease. Take Little Pete as a rather typical example.

Born Fung Jing Toy in 1865, Little Pete was brought from China to San Francisco by his father in 1870. The father wanted to prepare his son for the new world so he taught him English instead of Chinese. While well motivated the idea lacked practicality. The boy found himself growing up in Chinatown where few spoke English, but in time he overcame the handicap by employing an interpreter. And his command of English gave him a certain edge over his contemporaries. Beginning as an errand boy delivering shoes, he soon became a salesman and then a partner in the shoe business. By then Little Pete realized that there were shortcuts to success that had nothing to do with the Puritan Ethic so he abandoned the shoe business for the vice business.

Chinatown offered opportunities in gambling, opium, and yellow slavery. The Chinese, after all, were natural gamblers who might bet a fortune on the number of flies a dead fish would attract. Opium "dens" were less numerous than gambling joints, but they were plentiful, each equipped with private

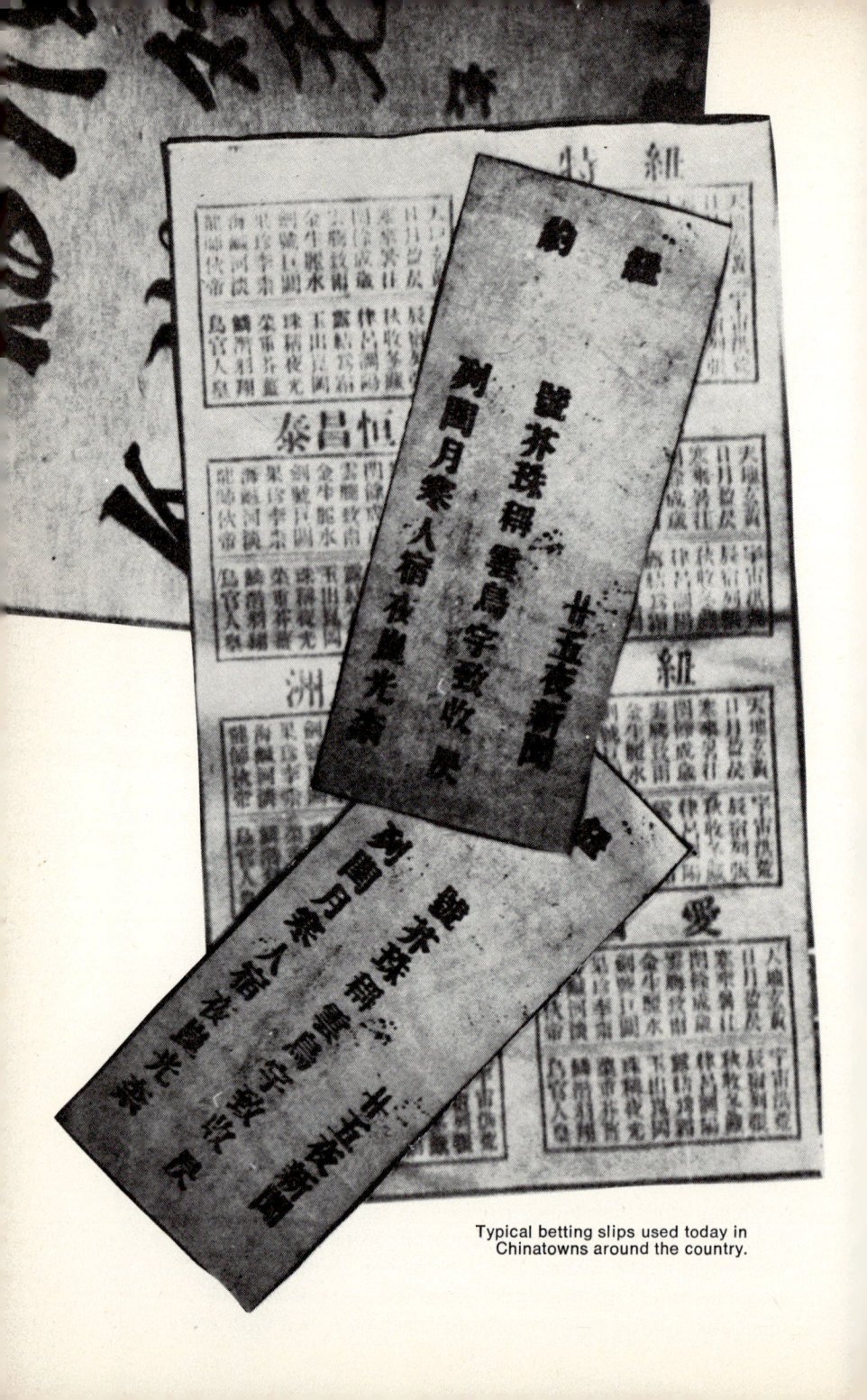

Typical betting slips used today in Chinatowns around the country.

booths where the happy smoker could take his ease while enjoying golden dreams. Many such places were closed to white men but as publicity made the existence of the "peculiar establishment" known, it became profitable to operate pseudo-dens for the benefit of the tourist. All of which helped make stories and movies about Fu Manchu popular later.

Slavery was the big business, however, and it was the taste of the white man for "yellow meat" which made it so. The girls, some just children, were bought wholesale from their fathers in China and brought to San Francisco by the boatload. There they were sold to the highest bidder. A "ripe and clean" girl of fourteen might bring as high as $300. Legally, she "sold" her services for five years, but the contracts were so worded that—like some modern contracts of loan sharks—the obligation never ended. The traffic was similar to the trade in young Jewesses being conducted in Chicago by such entrepreneurs as "Big Jim" Colosimo, but it differed in that individual merchants rather than gangs brought the girls in and retailed them. The price per trick was much smaller, ranging from fifty cents for men to twenty-five cents for high-school boys learning about life.

From the vice business as well as almost all other forms of enterprise in Chinatown, the tongs took tribute. Initially, the tong was somewhat similar to a labor union, but it quickly came to resemble a Mafia "family" as the need for strong leadership gave the unscrupulous their chance. Blood lines were important and provided the basic structure just as in the Mafia. An elaborate code complete with blood oaths and mumbo jumbo added to the sense of belonging and the general fun. There was, of course, no boss of bosses, and tong wars were frequent affairs as one leader sought to avenge his honor or extend his control at the expense of another. In the course of such battles the words "hatchet man" were added to the lexicon of politicians, journalists, and gangsters. The principal weapon of the salaried killers of the tongs was a hatchet, although they usually carried a couple of revolvers as well. The guns were used when the killer wanted to impress a crowd, but the hatchet at close range was more effective since the killer was a notoriously poor shot. To guard against hatchets, the top leaders of the tongs wore suits of chain mail under their silken gowns, and sometimes lined their caps with steel as well.

The tongs began in San Francisco and spread to other cities with large Chinese-American populations. In New York, wars between the tongs broke out a decade or two later than on the west coast, reflecting if nothing else the longer distance from China. As with the Mafia there was no organizational ties between tongs in different cities. In essence, each tong was but a "gang." It had more members than a Jesse James could recruit in the West, because the population was much more dense and the source of revenue more centralized. Moreover, since—like the Mafia in the beginning—the victims were of the same minority group as the predators, the ruling establishment could at first ignore them. Had Chris Evans and John Sontag robbed Chinese instead of railroads, they might have lived to become respected. Proof is in a statement given authorities by John's brother, George Sontag, who told of a time when Evans wanted a job "herding Chinese for the Southern Pacific." To show the need he "threw a couple of pretty good dynamite bombs into the Chinese sheds and then opened a couple of barrels of shot into them."

Little Pete had no minority race to kick around but he recognized that he could exploit his own people without interference from the white man. Taking his capital from the shoe business he invested in some gambling houses and won the backing of the Sum Yop Tong. By the time he was twenty-five, thanks to his knowledge of English and his insight into the American Way,

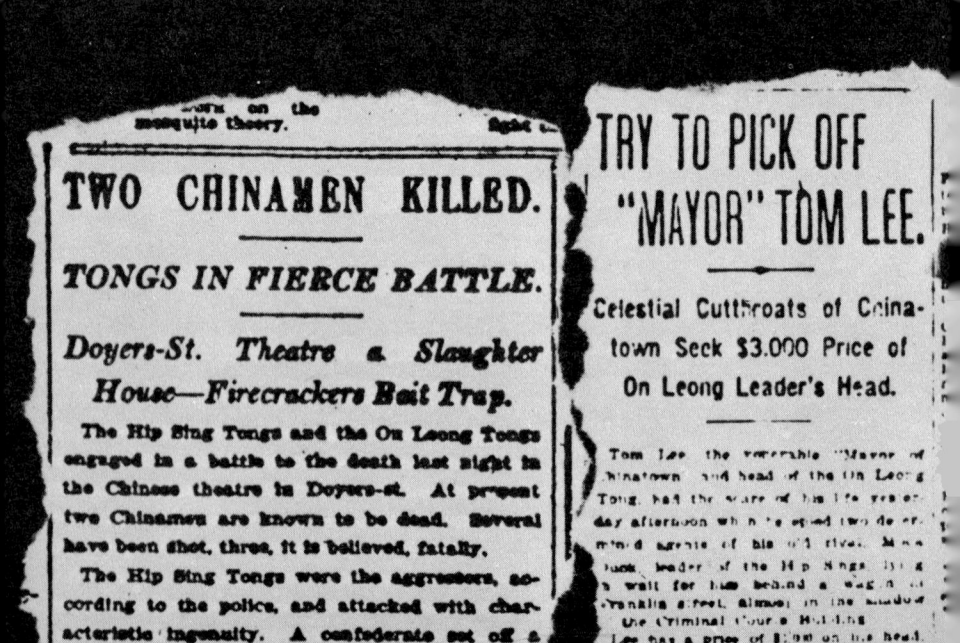

TWO CHINAMEN KILLED.

TONGS IN FIERCE BATTLE.

Doyers-St. Theatre a Slaughter House—Firecrackers Bait Trap.

The Hip Sing Tongs and the On Leong Tongs engaged in a battle to the death last night in the Chinese theatre in Doyers-st. At present two Chinamen are known to be dead. Several have been shot, three, it is believed, fatally.

The Hip Sing Tongs were the aggressors, according to the police, and attacked with characteristic ingenuity. A confederate set off a

TRY TO PICK OFF "MAYOR" TOM LEE.

Celestial Cutthroats of Chinatown Seek $3,000 Price of On Leong Leader's Head.

Tom Lee, the venerable "Mayor of Chinatown" and head of the On Leong Tong, had the scare of his life yesterday afternoon when he spied two determined agents of his old rival, Mock

he controlled the tong. War followed inevitably with the Sue Yop Tong and soon bodies were being chopped up all over Chinatown as Little Pete sought to become emperor in the west.

In such a world within a world as Chinatown it was easy for Little Pete to forget that his domain existed only at the sufferance of white men—police and politicians. Accustomed to paying off to operate gambling houses and vice dens, he forgot that murder fell into another classification. As a result of trying to bribe the district attorney to fix a murder case, he found himself in San Quentin for five years. But prison can mature an intelligent mind and Little Pete grew up. Released, he soon regained control of the Sum Yops and formed an alliance with "the blind white devil," as Chris Buckley, the political boss of San Francisco, was known. Buckley was blind but he helped Little Pete become the undisputed boss of Chinatown.

Power has its price, of course, and it can be doubted that a respectable western outlaw would have considered the rewards sufficient if he had to sleep each night in a windowless room with guard dogs chained on each side of the door, wear chain mail and a steel-lined hat, and go nowhere without white bodyguards walking ahead, behind, and at his side. But every man to his taste. Little Pete also employed a jewel-bearer to trot along with a casket full of diamond rings, gold watches, and platinum matchboxes. He wore a different suit each day, and he spent at least two hours each morning combing and oiling his queue. Grat Dalton would have considered Little Pete a "dude" and Little Pete would have thought Grat a barbarian; but Grat would have envied Little Pete his freedom to attend the races regularly and to bet as much as $8,000 each day. That seems a lot, yet, when one remembers that Grat bet his neck on his horse every time he robbed a bank it, perhaps, becomes somewhat incidental. And when one learns, as did racing officials in San Francisco, that Little Pete was fixing the races he bet on, the whole business loses its unique qualities. The Daltons were fixing races long before they robbed a bank.

Barred from the tracks, Little Pete turned to other ways of cheating. And soon his income aroused the Sue Yops to put a price of $3,000 on Little Pete's head. This was similar to the offers of some railroads to pay $1,000 for dead train robbers but not one cent for live ones. Immediately killers of twelve tongs began to stalk Little Pete looking for an opportunity. But the white bodyguards were well-paid and faithful. The professionals failed. As often happens, however, some amateurs who didn't understand the odds came along and made the project seem simple.

The heroes were Chew Tin Gop and Lem Jung, two prospectors who had struck it rich and were planning to go home to China. On January 23, 1897, they caught Little Pete in a barbershop—shades of Albert Anastasia—getting his queue washed and replaited. It was the evening of the Chinese New Year and Little Pete was in a hurry. He had come out in holiday mood and left his bodyguards behind.

Shoving the barber aside, Lem Jung grabbed his victim by the hair and shoved a revolver down his neck—inside the chain mail. At such close range not even a Chinaman could miss, but Lem Jung pulled the trigger five times just to make certain. He blasted Little Pete's spine into fragments. Unlike some "prices" allegedly put out by the Mafia, the assassins collected the promised reward and went home to China.

A wave of killings followed as the Sue Yops got a lot of revenge on the Sum Yops. It ended only when the Emperor of China intervened. All of the Sue Yop's relatives in China were rounded up and the tong in San Francisco was notified by cable that they would be executed if another Sum Yop was killed. That ended the slaughter.

Chinese laborers working for the Union Pacific Railroad.

The Sum Yops managed to give Little Pete a sendoff worthy of a Chicago hood. Three Chinese bands followed the hearse as firecrackers popped and black-robed priests shook rattles. About twenty wagons brought up the rear of the mile-long procession. They were loaded with baked meats, rice, gin, and tea and were intended to allow Little Pete's spirit some refreshment before it moved on to heaven. But, alas—a group of white devils hijacked the wagons and ate up all the food. Presumably Little Pete went hungry to his final destination—and some persons doubted it was heaven after all.

Some seventy years after Little Pete went to his reward, wherever it was, violence flared again in Chinatown. In the summer of '73, newspaper stories told of new gang warfare that had claimed fifteen lives. As UPI put it:

"The shootings have recalled the Chinatown tong wars of more than two generations ago, when rival groups battled with hatchets and knives over control of slavery of young women and gambling."

But in the interim no syndicate, no organized crime. Even those who in the past attempted to make much of the "Yellow Peril" would have difficulty in 1973 with Ngin Hoo, shot while carrying home a twenty-two-pound salmon given him by a friend.

* * * * *

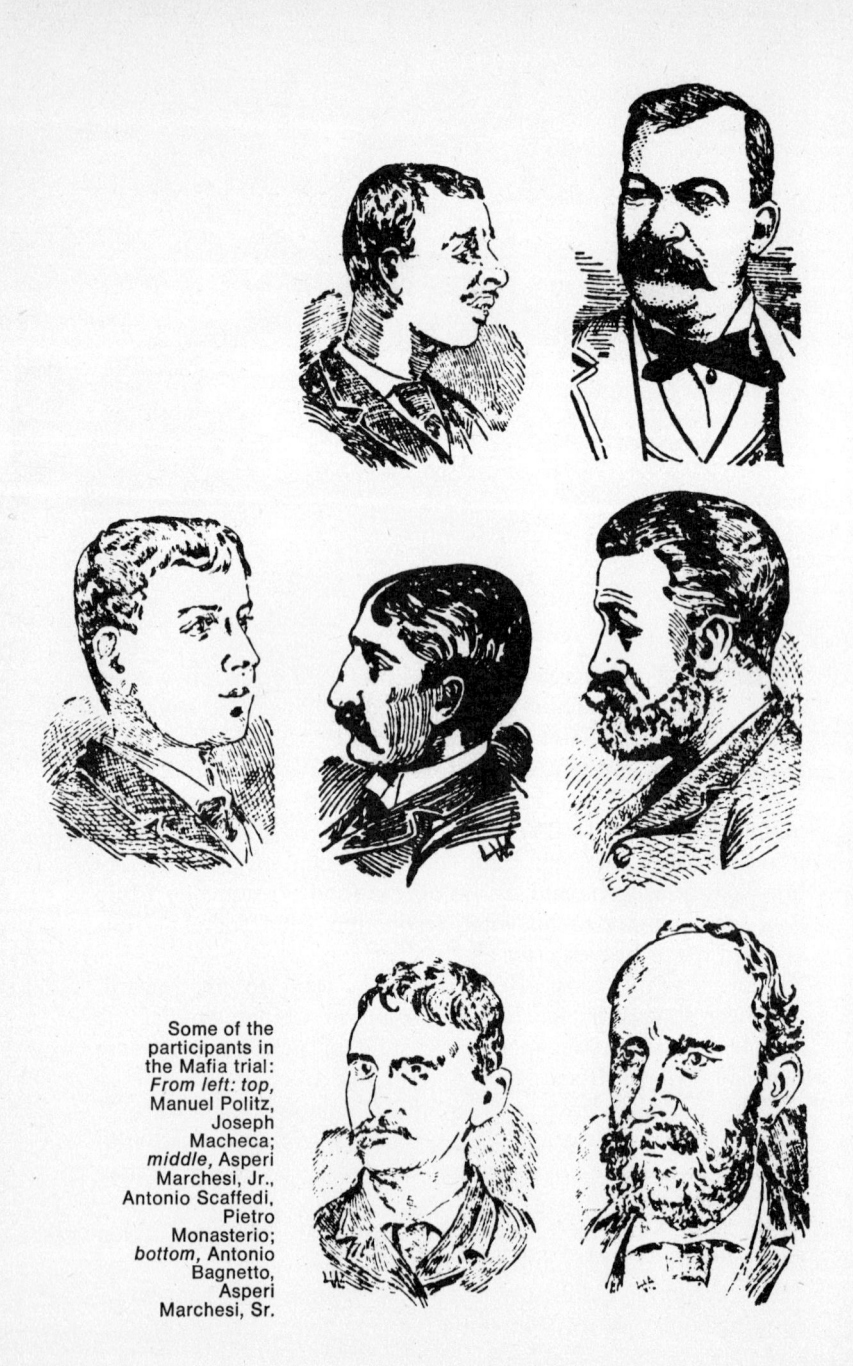

Some of the participants in the Mafia trial: *From left: top,* Manuel Politz, Joseph Macheca; *middle,* Asperi Marchesi, Jr., Antonio Scaffedi, Pietro Monasterio; *bottom,* Antonio Bagnetto, Asperi Marchesi, Sr.

So widely accepted has the legend become that today when one speaks of a Sicilian one thinks automatically of the Mafia. All of which may be fair enough so long as it is understood that there is a considerable difference in the concept of a vast, highly organized, secret society operating across international borders, and a gang of immigrants preying off of each other in an ethnic ghetto.

A lot of Sicilians reached New Orleans before and immediately after the Civil War. Like the Chinese in San Francisco and the Irish in Boston, they settled down to learn as fast as possible how to get ahead in the Land of Opportunity. The Ku Klux Klan became popular with wasp citizens during the bitterness of Reconstruction, so perhaps it isn't surprising that the Sicilians should form an ethnic version of their own. Modern Mafia experts have seized upon this development as the true beginning of Mafia power in the United States. If one accepts this version, the boys in New Orleans were almost too busy setting up chapters—families—in New York, San Francisco, and Chicago to have time to conduct business at home. It is a sinister picture and explains a lot. Unfortunately, for the legend buildlers, it is mostly after-the-fact romantic fiction.

In reality, the Sicilians in New Orleans acted pretty much like Sicilians everywhere. They were too busy fighting each other to have time for empire building across the nation. Vendetta followed vendetta, and bosses came and went. But so long as it was kept confined to the ghetto no one worried too much about it.

About 1885, the Matranga brothers became important. Charles and Tony had immagination—they introduced the practice of swearing blood oaths on human skulls with daggers sticking from the eye sockets—a mumbo jumbo Joseph Valachi would have appreciated. Rivals were the Provenzano brothers who had achieved a monopoly along the piers in the unloading of fruit ships from South America. (The same thing happened in other cities and is largely true today. Apparently the Mafia has an affinity for bananas.) The monopoly had brought the Provenzanos wealth, and wealth had brought them political influence. Among their buddies they numbered David Hennessy, the newly appointed chief of police.

The inevitable "war" followed as the Matrangas moved in on the Provenzanos, and bodies littered the streets. The favorite weapon was the sawed-off shotgun and it became to the Sicilians

TOBER 16, 1890.

ASSASSINATED

Superintendent of Police David C. Hennessy Victim of the Vendetta.

Ambuscaded at His Doorstep and Six Bullets Shot Into His Body, One of Which is Pronounced Fatal.

The Murderers Declared to be Italians of the Criminal Class.

The Chief Removed to the Charity Hospital in an Ambulance,

Where He is Visited by the Mayor and by His Aged Mother.

A Number of Suspects Promptly Placed in Arrest.

The Wounded Chief at 3 O'Clock This Morning Was Resting Easily.

- David C. Hennessy -

lar nature had been ...ed in the city during the preced... ...ars and the authorities with the undiv... support of all English-speaking citizens...

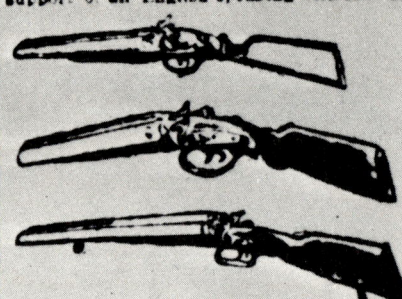

GUNS USED BY THE ASSASSINS AND F.UND IN THE GUTTER.

termined to make all p...ble efforts to stop this incessant sla... ...da Hen- ...ssy took...

THE HENNESSY CASE.

How the Assassins Were Apprised of the Coming of Their Victim.

The "Dago Whistle" Figures in the Case.

Joe Macheca Identified as the Lessee of the Monasterio Shanty.

His Ill-Feeling and Fear of Hennessy the Basis of Te...

WORK OF THE MAFIA.

Secretary Vandervoort's Narrative of the Late Chief's Experiences.

Why the Bandits Learned to Hate and Dread Him.

HENNESSY AND THE MAFIA.
The Recollections of the Secretary of the Chief of Police.
Mr. Geo. W. Vandervoort, Chief Hennessy's secretary and confidential friend knew a gre...

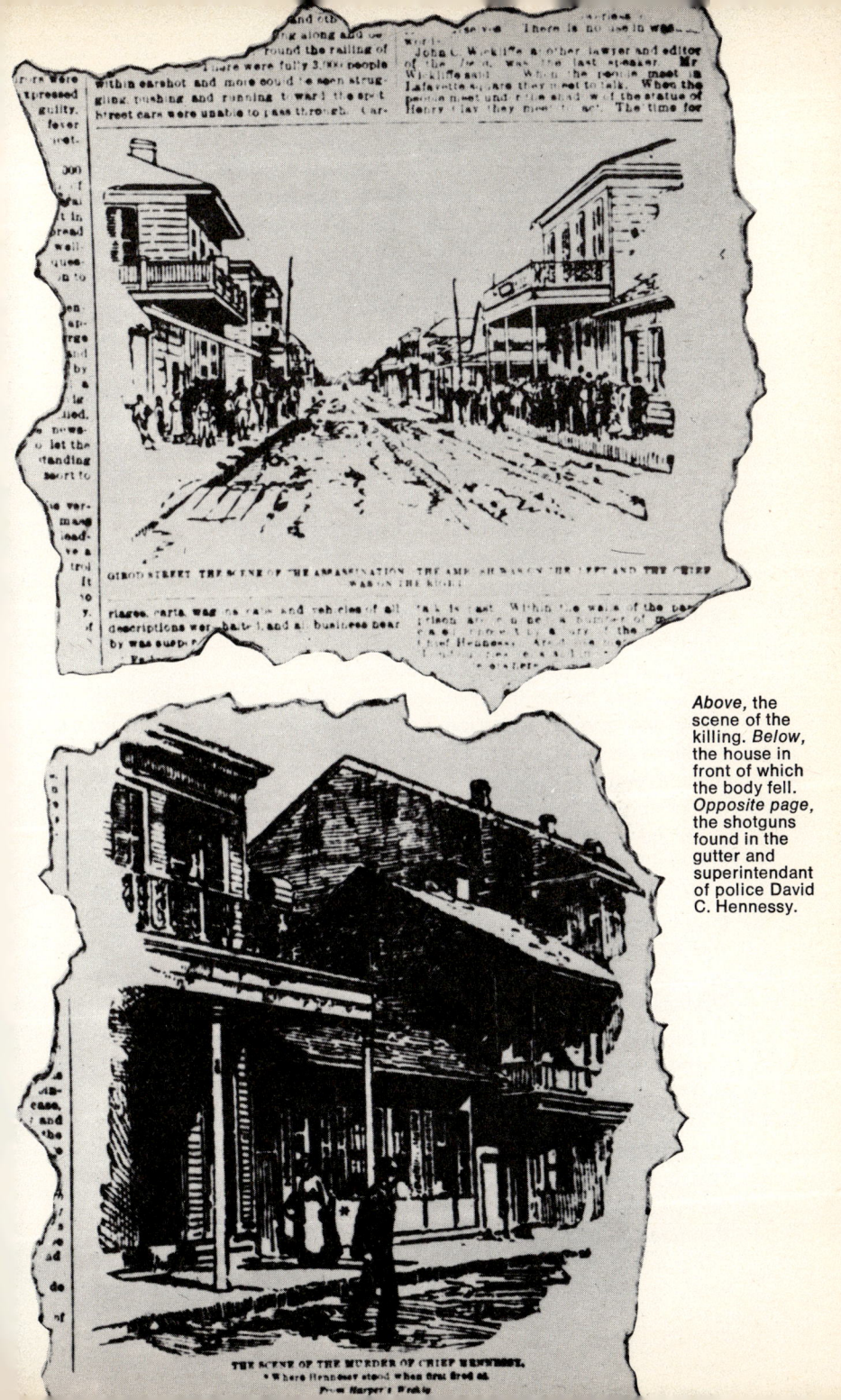

Above, the scene of the killing. *Below,* the house in front of which the body fell. *Opposite page,* the shotguns found in the gutter and superintendant of police David C. Hennessy.

what the hatchet was to the Chinese—at least in popular literature. The climatic battle came in April, 1890, when the Provenzanos ambushed Tony Matranga at the corner of Claiborne Avenue and Esplanade Street. The police picked up Joe and Peter Provenzano and several of their men. All of which made Chief Hennessy unhappy.

Trial was set for October. The Matrangas, apparently willing to settle the vendetta in the courts, contented themselves with hiring their own attorneys to aid in the prosecution. This upset Chief Hennessy even more. He held a press conference and announced that the Matrangas were not hardworking merchants like the Provenzanos but, in reality, members of an international secret society. Moreover, he said, he had written for supporting data from the police of Rome. When it arrived he would present it from the witness stand at the Provenzanos' trial.

The objective observer has some difficulty in understanding how this partisanship on the part of a police official can be so ignored by historians. The answer, of course, is the events that followed, which made it necessary for the Establishment to adopt the chief's prejudices as facts.

Two days before the trial began, on October 15, 1890, Hennessy was gunned down on Basin Street. A friend who heard the shots and was first on the scene reported that when he asked the conventional question:

"Who did it?"

Hennessy whispered,

"The Dagoes."

Whereupon, he fainted, dying the next day. A great wave of public indignation swept the city. A double-barreled shotgun was found and identified as the death weapon. And, of course, everyone knew that shotguns were Mafia weapons. Soon all New Orleans was singing:

> Chief Hennessy, he was murdered for no cause that we know,
> And the murderer in prison he will pine;
> Why men have such a will that for vengeance they can kill,
> Such men with Satan surely must combine.

A roundup began and before the month ended twenty-one "Dagoes" were arrested, of which nineteen were indicted. In retrospect, it seems like a lot of people for a single "hit," but the mood in New Orleans was the more the merrier. There was some talk of saving the state the expense of a trial, but cool heads prevailed. The trial began on February 16, 1891, and

Restraining Politz, one of the accused, during the trial.

in the process the state dropepd charges against two men and the judge directed a verdict of acquittal against Charles Matranga—surely the ringleader of the gang if public opinion was correct. This strange action was soon overshadowed when the jury said it was hopelessly divided on three men but in agreement that everyone else was innocent.

Now the song had an ironic sound with its promise that "the murderer in prison he will pine." And the good citizens of the town held a mass meeting in front of the statue of Henry Clay. There the organizers—described as "prominent citizens"— announced that justice demanded swift punishment. The crowd agreed and an "execution party" was formed. A gunshop was looted of rifles and, yes, shotguns, and in military style the group marched over to the jail with the mob following along behind in pride and anticipation.

Parish Prison at Congo Square kept its gates closed, but the

The mob fires at and kills nine prisoners in jail. They also hanged two prisoners outside the prison. These actions, which were cheered on by the police, created an international incident.

THE PEOPLE A MOB.

Eleven Prisoners Lynched in the New Orleans Jail.

LED BY LAWYERS AND MERCHANTS

Formed at the Foot of the Statue of Henry Clay.

THE POLICE CHEER THE MOB ON.

A CRY FOR REPARATION

New Orleans Quiet but Other Cities Agitated Over the Lynching.

AN INTERNATIONAL QUESTION.

Secretary Blaine Reminds Gov. Nicholls of Our Treaty With Italy.

"Constant Protection" Guaranteed to Italian Subjects—The President and Secretary of State Overwhelmed With Telegrams—The Italian Minister Makes Formal Protest—The Victims Buried

---

to the city it was distributed free headed:

EXTRA
of the
L'ECO D'ITALIA.

7 Sicilians Slaughtered AT NEW ORLEANS.

A CROWD OF PEOPLE PLUNDERS THE SHOPS OF THE GUN-SMITHS, ENTERS THE PRISON, DRAGS OUT 7 ACQUITTED SI-CILIANS, AND LYNCHES THEM

The first column and a half was devoted despatches on the subject, followed by a comment to the effect that it was shameful that such a thing should occur among a civilized people. Then came a stern arraignment of the people concerned under the heading:

SLAUGHTER OF THE INNOCENTS.

Frank Dimaio, one of the most brilliant Pinkerton operatives, in his "Mafia" uniform. He was instrumental in bringing the accused to trial. Later he followed Butch Cassidy and the Sundance Kid to South America.

vigilantes broke in through a rear door and began hunting down their victims. Eleven men had been selected as sufficient sacrifice to the ghost of Hennessy. Seven of them were shot down in the prison yard. Two more were found hiding and were blasted. For the enjoyment of the mob outside the walls, two others were pulled into the streets and hanged in old West— or new South—style.

Triumphantly everyone returned to Henry Clay and heard a promise from the prominent citizens that should the Sicilians fail to heed the message it would be repeated. Immediately a new ballad was born, the last verse of which proclaimed:

> Great praise is due those gentlemen whom we all do know,
> Who called upon the citizens for them their powers to show.
> No more assassins we will have sent from a foreign soil,
> In New Orleans we've proved to all we're honest sons of toil.

Not everyone agreed. And as criticism mounted in other cities and in Italy, the people of New Orleans rallied and stood firm. The concept of the Mafia as a foreign secret society became accepted as gospel, and for years writers have exulted that the slaughter in Parish Prison broke the Mafia in New Orleans. All of which was a lot of nonsense.

Despite the assurances of the members of the Cotton, Sugar, and Stock Exchanges, the scandal wouldn't go away. The Italian government withdrew its ambassador and broke diplomatic relations. War threatened. Finally, the United States agreed to pay $20,000 in reparations, and the Italians dropped their demand for an investigation which might have exposed the "Mafia Menace" as a fraud.

Ironically, something similar happened in 1963 on a national scale when the FBI was forced into battle against organized crime and conveniently discovered "La Cosa Nostra." It made good copy, as the newspapermen say, so it was immediately exploited and the concept of the "godfather" became as embedded in our Mafia mythology as the heroic figure of Chief Hennessy. After all it diverted attention from those with better political connections, and that was justification enough.

* * * * *

Charles Dion O'Banion and his wife Viola. Choir boy, singing waiter, enforcer for William Randolph Hearst's *Herald Examiner*, O'Banion headed a gang of notorious mobsters that included some of the most vicious thieves, safecrackers, and murderers of the day, among them George "Bugs" Moran and Earl "Hymie" Weiss. He operated a flower shop that supplied most of the decorations for the splashy gangster funerals of the 1920s. He was killed among his flowers in 1924.

In 1892, the year Bob and Grat Dalton died at Coffeyville, an immigrant Irish house-painter became a father in Aurora, Illinois. Before the baby could walk, the father moved to an Irish shantytown on Chicago's North Side. A wave of Sicilians crowded in and the area became known variously as "Little Sicily" and "Little Hell." The baby grew into boyhood and fell off a streetcar injuring his leg. Thereafter he was known as "Gimpy"—until such familiarity became downright dangerous.

Charles Dion O'Banion was a pious boy despite his surroundings, and the Irish priests at Holy Name Cathedral had hopes he might discover a vocation. For four years he was a choirboy, but then his voice changed and so did his ambitions. As a leader in a juvenile band known as the Market Street Gang, he defended the Irish against the Sicilians. So strong were the prejudices developed during this youthful phase that ultimately they were to make history in Chicago.

Of course Dion's boys did more than fight Sicilians—they were stealing everything not nailed down. Yet it was his training in the choir that stood him in good stead when he took his first job indoors. He was hired as a singing waiter in McGovern's Saloon. When he sang "Mother Machree," he could bring blinding tears to the most cynical drunk—a circumstance that made it a lot easier for Dion to pick the drunk's pocket.

Newspaper wars in Chicago—as in Cleveland and New York —proved a fine training school for future gangsters, and O'Banion graduated with honors. He hired out his gang to one side and then another in the fight to boost circulation by eliminating the competition. The gang branched out into highway robbery and safecracking, but O'Banion had a habit of using too much dynamite. Sometimes he blew up the building instead of the safe. Yet he enjoyed the noise and could be as philosophical as those members of the Wild Bunch who blasted a safe so thoroughly they shredded the $50,000 it contained.

The gang that emerged—growing up with Dion—was largely Irish. But along with such men as Handsome Dan McCarthy were Cowboy Alterie, who actually owned a ranch in Colorado, and Nails Morton, who had a Croix de Guerre from service in France. Morton, however, is remembered primarily because he visited the Cowboy's ranch and learned to ride. Upon returning to Chicago, he was thrown from a horse in Lincoln Park and kicked to death. O'Banion led a firing squad to the stables and took the horse for a walk. The execution was celebrated at a wild party and was immortalized in the movie, *Public Enemy*, starring James Cagney and Jean Harlow.

Hymie Weiss (Wajiechowski) was O'Banion's chief lieutenant. George "Bugs" Moran ranked next. Like Weiss, Moran was of Polish extraction, and he was married to a full-blooded Sioux Indian. It was a mixed bunch that O'Banion gathered around him, composed as it was of every nationality except, of course, Sicilian.

With the coming of Prohibition things began to change. There was pressure in Chicago and elsewhere for an end to independent action by individual gangs. This pressure would ultimately produce an organization capable of enforcing its will and, in effect, organizing crime. But the process of consolidation was a complicated one, especially in Chicago which prided itself—and still does—on the maverick nature of its fast-buck boys. Some of O'Banion's exploits deservedly rank with those of Jesse James. Take, for example, the time he led his gang into the West Side railroad yards and robbed a train of—not cash or gold dust but $100,000 of Canadian whiskey. Then there was the time he looted a warehouse of almost two thousand barrels of bonded whiskey, replacing the liquor with water to delay detection.

The Earl "Hymie" Weiss funeral entourage. Thousands of dollars were spent on floral pieces for mobster funerals of the period.

Still despite all these glorious achievements, despite the fact that the chief of police estimated he was responsible for the murder of "at least twenty-five men," O'Banion is remembered today as Chicago's most famous florist. He was half-owner of a flower shop on State Street located across the boulevard from the cathedral where he had sung in the choir as a boy. Nor was the flower shop just a front for his illegal activities—he loved flowers and worked regularly among them. Moreover, such was his standing that no gangster could be decently buried without scores of suitable floral tributes from O'Banion's shop. It became a ritual, the gangster funeral, as every punk from Al Capone down sought to display his big heart (and pocketbook) in an orgy worthy of the sentimental folks of show business. All of which meant money in the pocket for O'Banion who hauled in the extra blossoms for each occasion by train from New York.

Like Jesse James, O'Banion loved only one woman and she responded with loyalty and affection. Dion, she was fond of telling reporters, never left home without kissing her goodbye. On one such morning the gunman was crossing a street when a car backfired. He jerked out a revolver and fired at the only man in sight—a laborer on his way to work. The unfortunate was wounded in the leg, and O'Banion felt so sorry about it he sent a box of cigars to the hospital. Then he went home to his wife and the player piano he loved.

Why was O'Banion so nervous? Well, there could have been many reasons but the "Terrible Gennas" were enough. There were six Genna brothers, Sicilians, and the only thing they had in common with the Irish O'Banion was religious zeal. That is to say they carried crucifixes as routinely as pistols, and went to church regularly. Five of the brothers have been described as "typical Sicilian killers—haughty, overbearing, contemptuous, savage, treacherous . . ." well, the idea comes through. The sixth brother was "Tony the Aristocrat," a patron of the opera and a student of architecture. Tony lived apart from the family, but he was always on hand when a decision on who to murder was made. Also present at such solemn occasions were two "hit men," John Scalisi and Albert Anselmi, whose contribution to culture consisted of the theory that by spreading garlic on bullets one could give the victim gangrene.

All in all, the Gennas were enough to annoy a man who had never cared for Sicilians in the first place. For one couldn't overlook them. Whereas O'Banion had gone into the liquor business on the basis of honesty—the best bonded whiskey he could steal—the Gennas had introduced the practice of making

Right, a rare picture of Johnnie Torrio in the early 1920s. *Opposite page*, two purported killers of O'Banion: John Scalise and Albert Anselm, associates of the Genna gang.

rotgut in backroom stills and had set every Italian-Sicilian in the Taylor Street area to making it. The Gennas bottled it as Scotch or brandy or bourbon—according to the demand—and began flooding the North Side with it. Annoyed, O'Banion hijacked a Genna truck loaded with $30,000 worth of "Old Palermo," and spilled it on the street.

John Torrio, the emerging mastermind of Chicago crime, tried to stop a war and was temporarily successful. But O'Banion never really bought Torrio's concept of a crime syndicate composed of previously independent gangs, and soon he broke completely with Al Capone's mentor. More than that, he added insult to injury by selling Torrio his interest in a brewery he knew was about to be raided by police. Under the circumstances one can understand why Torrio—a product of New York's "Hell's Kitchen" decided the Irishman was a throwback to the dark ages. O'Banion responded with one of the most famous lines in the history of crime:

"Tell them Sicilians to go to hell."

For the record, it has also been quoted as:

"To hell with them Sicilians."

The death of Mike Merlo, respected head of Unione Siciliano —the name "Mafia" was never popular in Chicago and no one ever heard of "La Cosa Nostra"—kept O'Banion busy in his flower shop for the next few days. He was there alone on November 10, 1924, having filled Torrio's $10,000 order and Capone's

The "Terrible" Gennas and their families. *Left to right*, Sam, Angelo, Peter, Tony, and Jim. Angelo, Tony, and Mike, who does not appear in the picture, were killed.

DEATH MARKED FOR 3 MORE OF GENNA FAMILY

Police Told Mafia Is Back of Killings.

Chicago Daily Tribune
THE WORLD'S GREATEST NEWSPAPER

LXXXIV—NO. 163   THURSDAY, JULY 9, 1925.—56 PAGES   PRICE TWO CENTS

NNAS IN TERROR; TONY DIE

NEWS SUMMARY

BRYAN TACTICS PLACE SCOPES DEFENSE IN HOLE

Colby Withdraws from Trial.

BY PHILIP KINSLEY

HE'S ALWAYS SEEING THINGS

U. S. at Loss to Find Cells for Its Felons

THIRD VICTIM NAMES SLAYER IN DYING

Sam Begs Brother to Aid Police

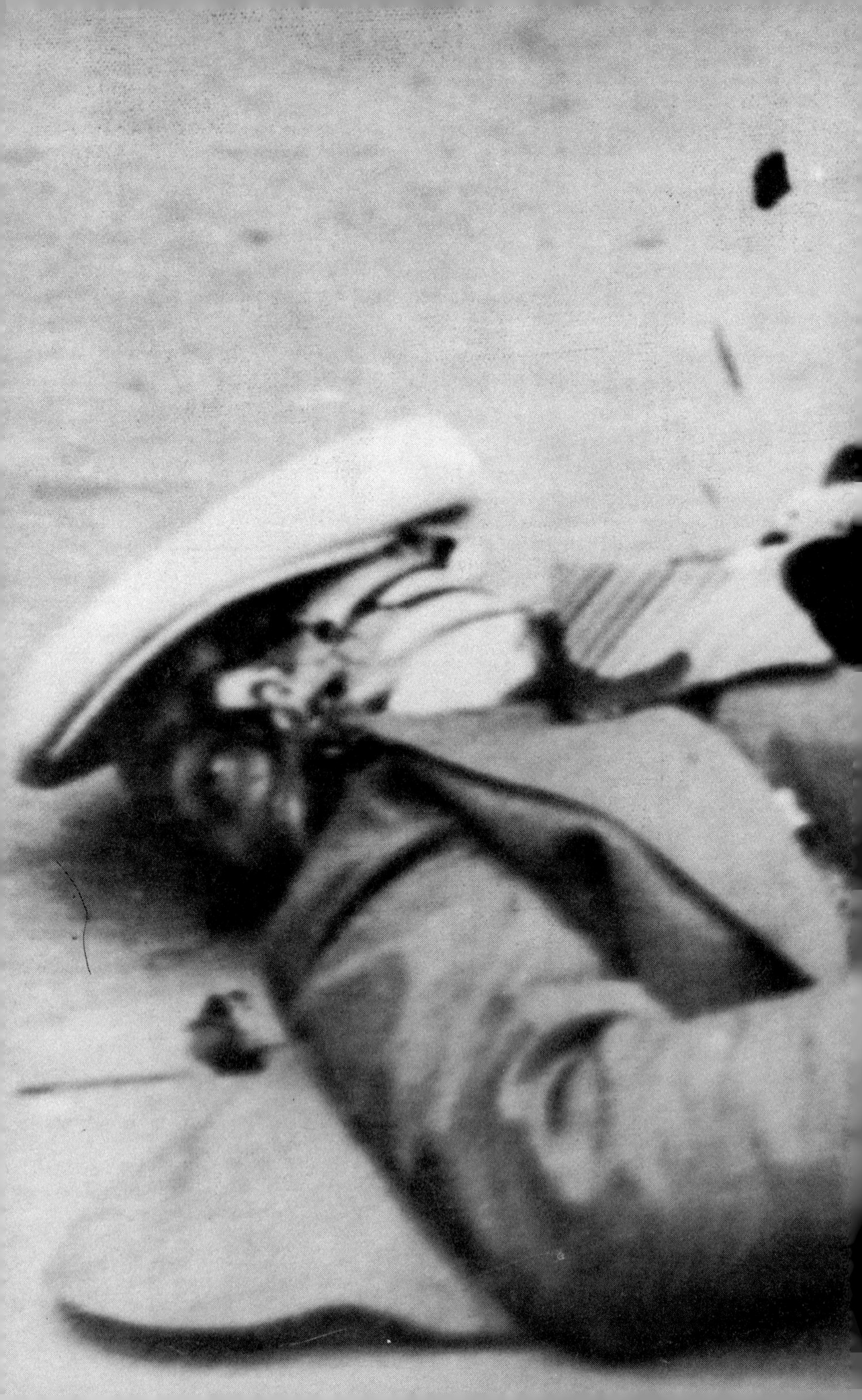

Opposite page, the bloodied head of Earl "Hymie" Weiss after he was gunned down in the street by purported members of the Genna mob. *Above,* the beginning of Weiss's funeral.

HYMIE WEISS SLAIN; O'BRIEN, ATTORNEY, HIT

Machine Gun Blast Rakes Street.

(Pictures on back page.)

Machine gun fire blazed again in gang warfare yesterday afternoon in North State street across the street from Holy Name cathedral, the death toll and the list of wounded being:

THE DEAD.

EARL "HYMIE" WEISS, successor as gang leader to Dean O'Banion and shot down at almost the same spot as O'Banion.

PATRICK MURRAY, brother to and

Top, Mike Genna and friend Germaine Triest. *Below*, George "Bugs" Moran and his wife. Involved in dozens of killings during the Prohibition Era, Moran's gang was wiped out at the St. Valentine's Day massacre.

$8,000 purchase of red roses. Ready to be picked up was a wreath ordered by Angelo Genna.

Three men entered the shop from a car parked across the street. There were at least six shots. Dion O'Banion was found amid his disarrayed flowers—carnations, liles, peonies—which he had knocked to the floor as he fell. There were six bullets in him, the last one fired into the base of his brain at close range. They gave Dion a worthy funeral—according to a respected judge, it was "one of the most nauseating things I've ever seen happen in Chicago." And Dion, the ex-choirboy, was buried next to the grave of a bishop. Twenty-six cars and trucks were needed to carry the flowers.

Hymie Weiss took over the O'Banion gang and promptly proved that non-Sicilians knew the meaning of vendetta. He led a party that wrecked Angelo Genna's car and blasted Angelo with sawed-off shotguns as he lay in the wreckage. (In Chicago sawed-off shotguns were NOT automatically classed as "Mafia weapons.") The Gennas tried to strike back. They ambushed Bugs Moran, wounding him, but in their getaway they were chased by cops. When the getaway car was wrecked—apparently the automobile presented problems to the Sicilians—the Gennas killed a cop. That was a mistake even in Chicago, and Mike Genna was hunted down and killed by other bluecoats a few minutes later. Tony the Aristocrat was next. Lured to a rendezvous, he was shot in the back five times at close range. The surviving Gennas fled to Sicily and other isolated hiding places.

Tony and Angelo were buried in the same cemetery holding Dion O'Banion, causing some anonymous wag to predict that there would be hell to pay on Judgment Day when the three graves were opened. Presumably the boys would come out shooting.

Men were just as violent, just as greedy, just as vindictive in rural America as in the cities, but in the wide open spaces, at least, there weren't so many of them and legend had room to grow.

John Dillinger in his youth. *Above*, at age three with his sister Audrey; *below*, as a teenager with his father in Indiana.

4

He Lost It at the Movies

AMERICANS FOR REASONS not clear like to explain their heroes by exploring their childhoods.

There is the story of one boy in kneepants who, having read and heard of the Teapot Dome scandal of the Harding days, assured his mother that he would grow up to become an honest lawyer.

His name was Richard M. Nixon.

Then there was the little boy out in Indiana who went alone to Sunday School. Someone asked:

"Where is your mother?"

"She's gone to heaven," the boy replied, "and some day I'm going up there to see her."

His name was John H. Dillinger.

He was born in the Oak Hill section of Indianapolis on June 22, 1903. His father, John, was a prosperous grocer who dabbled in real estate and, as they say in the Bible Belt, feared God. His mother, Mary, had waited fourteen years after the birth of her first child, Audrey, to risk her health for a son. She never fully recovered and died some three years after John's arrival. But Audrey carried on the crusade to make the boy a sincere Christian and well-mannered. In the latter she succeeded. His Sunday School teacher later recollected that he always tipped his hat to her.

The boy attended school until he was fourteen, distinguishing himself neither in the classroom nor on the athletic field. He liked things mechanical but he was a lousy shot; he enjoyed fighting, baseball, and playing cops and robbers. Upon leaving school he worked at several places before finding a job in a machine shop which paid well enough for him to buy a car.

His father watched all this with a heavy heart. When it

Above, Dillinger (*extreme left*) with friends when he served briefly on the battleship *Utah*. *Below*, at age nineteen.

became apparent he could no longer control his son in town, he sold his store and bought a sixty-acre farm near Mooresville, about twenty-five miles southwest of town. It was his fond belief that men who toiled the land were closer to God than those who sweated over man-made machinery in the city. Unhappily, the son really didn't care whether he was close to God or not. Getting up at 4:30 A. M. to slop the hogs was something less than inspiring. Soon he was driving into town after work. Mooresville's fleshpots were few and limited in attractions, but there was a poolhall where all the would-be wise guys congregated.

This slide downhill was checked momentarily when young John fell in love. The girl was the daughter of a leading citizen of Mooresville and was, of course, quite young. As soon as her parents learned of the affair, they moved quickly to terminate it. The suitor was made aware in terms quite specific that he was entirely unsuitable. He not only had no means of supporting the young lady but there was nothing in his background to indicate he had any prospects of so doing.

A conventional young man so far, Dillinger did the conventional romantic thing. Not having the Foreign Legion handy, he joined the Navy. To do that he had to lie about his age. Reminded of his father, he sent a postcard from Brooklyn and boarded the battleship *Utah* in the hope it would take him to far away places. It took him, instead, to Boston's Scollay Square. Dillinger became so delighted with the off-beat pleasures of that Puritan town, that he forgot to rejoin his ship when his liberty expired. The *Utah* sailed off without him, and Dillinger was abruptly a deserter. The *Utah* came to an unhappy end eighteen years and three days later at Pearl Harbor, but Dillinger didn't last so long.

It was cold in Boston and the shore patrol was active so Dillinger bummed his way back to Indiana and his father's farm. Soon the pattern repeated itself: he neglected his farm chores to hang around the pool hall, he fell in love with another fair, young (sixteen) maiden, and her parents objected. But perhaps they lacked the clout of the other family and when John assured them he would settle down and provide, objections were withdrawn. The marriage took place on April 12, 1924, and the ex-sailor had vindicated himself.

For that is what it amounted to. John had wanted to prove that he could get married, just as earlier he had sought to beat

John Dillinger (*back row, second from right*) with the Martinsville, Indiana, baseball team. His first associate in crime, Edgar Singleton, is in the front, first from the left.

up any school chum who had worsted him. Having enjoyed his triumph, he let Beryl sit at home—on his father's farm or in his father-in-law's residence in Martinsville. Some five months after marrying, he pulled his first robbery in conjunction with a poolroom pal, Edgar Singleton, who had recently graduated from Indiana State Prison.

It wasn't exactly a well-planned, professional job. More of a mugging, actually The two men were half-drunk when they got their bright idea, and they wasted no time. Their target was B. F. Morgan, a prosperous grocer. That much seems certain. But, unhappily, the details are less specific. It would appear that crime reporting in Mooresville left something to be desired. In any case Dillinger hit the elderly Morgan on the head—with a lead pipe or a heavy bolt or something—and knocked him down. In the fallen man's pocket was $550—a fortune to young Dillinger. Several night owls heard him singing later as he walked home to his father's farm.

On the advice of his father to plead guilty and take his medicine, John confessed when arrested and implicated Singleton. Ironically, he was sentenced to serve from ten to twenty-one years while Singleton, who pleaded not guilty to a different judge, was sentenced to from two to fourteen years. Even the senior Dillinger had trouble understanding the ways of justice

Dillinger in prison in Michigan City, Indiana, in 1929.

after that. He was later to stoutly maintain that his son's career in crime stemmed from the anger created by this "raw deal." Certainly, the anger kept the first-termer in constant trouble whereas the veteran Singleton played it cool and was paroled after only two years.

Despite written assurances from John that "we will be so happy when I can come to you and chase your sorrows away," Beryl, the child-bride, filed suit for divorce three days before her fifth wedding anniversary. She promptly remarried. Shortly after the divorce became final, Dillinger requested and received a transfer to the penitentiary at Michigan City. His official excuse—the baseball team was better and he was a potential big leaguer. The real reason—a desire to move up to the big time as far as felons were concerned. Obviously, Dillinger had decided on his future course of action—and the determining factor was Beryl. Later that year he wrote to his favorite niece, Mary:

"I do believe in God, but His ways seem strange to me sometimes."

Nine years after he was sentenced, Dillinger was at last paroled. His father was responsible, drawing up a petition and personally circulating it throughout the county. The judge signed it, the prosecutor signed it, and even the victim—Morgan—

125

signed. He got home on May 22, 1933, an hour after his stepmother died. The event so saddened the visitor that he attended church on Father's Day and sat through a sermon on the Prodigal Son, but his mind was on other things.

A lot had happened while Dillinger had been out of action. Babe Ruth had hit sixty homers in one year and the stock market had crashed in one day. The Republicans who had preached "America First" and unlimited prosperity were out of office, and the New Deal was enjoying its famous one hundred days of frenzied activity. The Depression hung heavily across the land and a lot of banks were closed.

Yet Dillinger's decision to turn bank robber cannot be blamed on economic conditions. Nor was he a Robin Hood in any sense of the word. He wanted money for its own sake and he wanted to make it as quickly, and as easily, as possible. In Michigan City he had learned a lot, and he wasted little time in putting it to use.

After a few warmup jobs to get the feel of things, he robbed the Dalesville, Indiana, bank on July 17, 1933. The loot totaled only $3,500, but Dillinger was satisfied. Assembling a team, he launched a *blitzkrieg* which soon had old-timers recalling the days of Jesse James. The First National Bank of Montpelier, Indiana, provides an example of his methods.

On August 4, 1933, near the close of banking hours, Dillinger and two companions drove up to the bank and parked. Dillinger left one man at the wheel and took the other one into the bank. While his companion kept customers and bank officials under control, Dillinger jumped the guard rail and scooped up cash into a sugar sack. The cashier was forced to open a small safe, and some $10,000 was taken. They fled to the car without firing a shot and made a clean getaway before police from neighboring towns set up roadblocks.

It was all very easy. Encouraging, almost. In three months he allegedly achieved a fortune of $100,000, and was beginning to talk of retirement in South America. All he needed was the right girl to take along. He had a possibility in hand—a girl named Mary who seemed congenial and was willing to divorce her husband in order to snare the suddenly famous Dillinger. On September 21, 1933, two weeks after he had taken the Massachusetts State Bank in Indianapolis for $24,000, he was sharing a room in Dayton, Ohio with Mary when the cops interrupted. The bandit surrendered without a fight. On his person

An FBI "Wanted" notice and the gun found on Dillinger's body when he was killed after leaving the Biograph Theater in July, 1934.

they found $2,604 and a sketch of a prison identifiable as the one at Michigan City. Was Dillinger masterminding a prison break for some of his old cellmates? How silly can one get?

Four days after his arrest, ten of his buddies broke out of Indiana State Prison at Michigan City. It was later proven that Dillinger had smuggled in the weapons that made the break possible. The boys were grateful. As Dillinger himself put it: "I stick to my friends and they stick to me."

It was sixteen days before the escaped prisoners got around to helping their benefactor. He had been transferred to the Allen County Jail in Lima, Ohio, where he told his cellmate he expected to be rescued. Shortly after supper a shot rang out in the office outside the cell block. Without a word, Dillinger put on his coat and stood waiting.

The shot was fired into the stomach of Sheriff Jesse L. Sarber by one of three men who walked in, identified themselves as Michigan police officers, and pulled guns when asked for credentials. The lawman was fatally wounded but made a gallant attempt to rise. The effort won him a pistol-whipping which laid his scalp open to the bone. Mrs. Sarber produced the keys to the cells. When the last door was open, Dillinger stepped out. The sheriff's wife was pushed inside along with a deputy. Leaving the sheriff dying on the floor, Dillinger and his allies hurried outside where two cars waited. By the time pursuit was mounted the gang had vanished into the night. Two days later two members reappeared long enough to raid the police station at Auburn, Indiana. They were after arms, not money, and the loot included revolvers, rifles, shotguns, one submachine gun, three bulletproof vests, and a lot of ammunition. Six days later a similar haul was made at the police station in Peru, Indiana, and, abruptly, panic gripped the state.

It often happens that when outlaws—be they on horseback or jet—achieve sensational success the reason is less their intelligence and skill than it is the stupidity and inefficiency of the forces of law and order. So it was with the police agencies of the midwest which were geared to fight off the Dalton boys had they suddenly reappeared, but were woefully unprepared to combat motorized gangs. Into this emergency came the FBI eventually. All the while loudly proclaiming faith in the superiority of local law enforcement, the special agents developed modern techniques and a ruthlessness that more than matched the enemy. Ironically, the FBI rested on its laurels and was soon

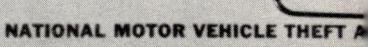

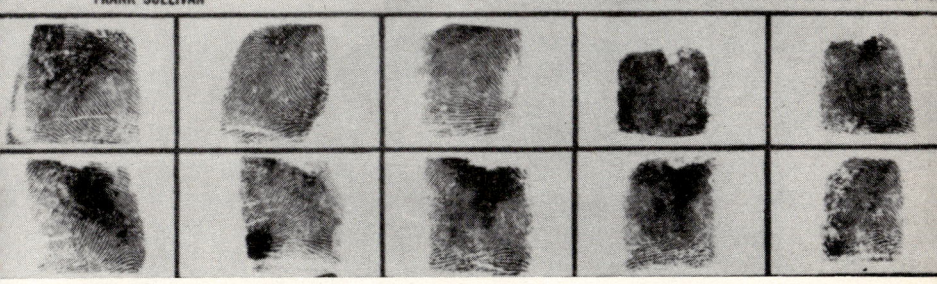

Top, fingerprints taken from Dillinger after he was slain. *Below*, fingerprints taken before he escaped with his wooden gun from the Crown Point, Indiana, jail. Despite his use of acid to alter his prints, experts identified his markings.

as incapable of fighting the more sophisticated menace of organized crime as the sheriffs had been incapable of battling bank robbers.

No one was admitting anything, however, in the weeks after Dillinger's escape from jail. Indiana lawmen kept their courage up whenever a week would pass without a new robbery by insisting that things had become too hot for the rascals and they had discreetly left the country. Meanwhile, just in case, they added steel bars and armor plate to police stations to keep the criminals out. Armored cars with machine guns were put on patrol in Indianapolis and a campaign started to equip police stations with one-way radio sets to facilitate the spread of alarms. The American Legion offered to arm its 30,000 members in Indiana and assign them to patrol the highways as mobile vigilantes. Not to be outdone, the National Guard promised to use tanks, airplanes, and poison gas if necessary. And the FBI, taking the first tentative step, instructed its agents in Cincinnati to help police if so requested.

Meanwhile, Dillinger went up to Chicago to enjoy a new girlfriend and catch up on all the movies he had missed. The newsreels were always interesting.

The new girl was Evelyn Frechette, an eighteen-year-old lass fresh off the Chippewa Indian Reservation at Neopit, Wisconsin. Dillinger met her at a nightclub where she was working as hatcheck girl while waiting for her husband to get out of jail. He spent so much money on her it became necessary to interrupt the vacation and recoup.

On November 20, 1933, the gang hit the American Bank and Trust Company of Racine, Wisconsin. As if in a holiday mood, they drove a blue and yellow sedan in contrast to the dark vehicles traditionally employed. Four men went inside the bank and a fifth parked the car out back. An indication of the times was the failure of the head teller, Harold Graham, to react when a man walked up to his window and said, "Hands up." Graham thought somebody was trying to be funny and went right on counting his cash preparatory to closing for the day. He was disillusioned when the stranger shot him in the arm. The bullet ranged down into his hip and Graham fell to the floor, still bewildered. He was not so bewildered, however, that he didn't remember to push the alarm button with his left hand. That didn't prevent one of the robbers from looting his cubicle, but it may have been responsible for the robber missing fifty

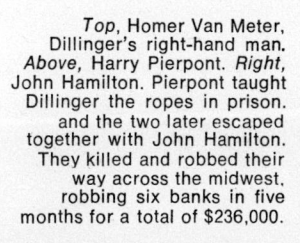

Top, Homer Van Meter, Dillinger's right-hand man. *Above*, Harry Pierpont. *Right*, John Hamilton. Pierpont taught Dillinger the ropes in prison, and the two later escaped together with John Hamilton. They killed and robbed their way across the midwest, robbing six banks in five months for a total of $236,000.

John Herbert Dillinger

$1,000 bills stashed at the back of a cash drawer. The police—accustomed now to false alarms—didn't take this latest one seriously until arriving at the bank. A gun battle broke out similar to some in which the James boys figured. Using hostages as shields, the men forced their way out to the car and escaped, taking two hostages with them. Some thirty-five miles down the road they stopped to refuel—a can of gasoline had been planted in advance—and released the hostages. Meanwhile, a painter continued working behind the bank. Asked why he didn't stop when the shooting started, the stolid German, a former soldier in East Prussia, replied:

"The shooting wasn't none of my business."

With $28,000 in the till it was possible to resume the vacation. Dillinger and Evelyn drove to Daytona Beach, Florida, and other members of the gang joined them. There was one bad moment when they found the lobby of the hotel swarming with police, who were there, it developed, only because someone had committed suicide. Dillinger and his latest love took in the air races at Miami and he gave her a diamond ring for Christmas. Unhappily, she celebrated too freely and got drunk. Dillinger, who was rather straitlaced, sent her back to Wisconsin. Came the new year and the boys fired submachine guns into the ocean in lieu of firecrackers.

It was a lot of fun, but Dillinger was lonesome without his Indian maid. He sent her a message to meet him in Chicago. The weather was bad and plans were made to finish the winter in Tucson, Arizona, a resort area future gangsters would exploit as a Miami-Beach-by-the-desert. But why not pick up some more cash before departing the combat zone?

A three-man job was set up for the First National Bank of East Chicago, Indiana. One man remained outside at the wheel of the car while Dillinger and one other entered the bank. John was carrying a trombone case containing a machine gun. Once inside, he opened the case and pointed the weapon while his companion began looting the money cages. An alarm button was pushed and cops began congregating outside the door. Unperturbed, Dillinger ordered his aide to get all the money. "We'll kill these coppers and get away. Take your time."

When some $20,000, was collected the two men started out, pushing two hostages ahead of them. Officer William O'Malley got a clear shot at Dillinger and hit him four times in the chest.

Dillinger was unhurt—the stolen bulletproof vest he was wearing stopped the slugs as it was supposed to do. In reply, he fired a burst from his submachine gun. O'Malley fell and the bandit fired again for good measure. The second burst killed the policeman.

The killing was the first and only one credited to Dillinger personally, and his family maintained that the credit was misapplied. Dillinger assured them, they later reported, that he never killed anyone.

While it is possible that this version is correct—Dillinger and other notorious criminals were blamed for a lot of things they didn't do—it seems unlikely. Identification was pretty certain. Chances are Dillinger was trying to spare his father the ultimate agony of knowing his son was a killer.

In full view of seven guns, Dillinger raced for the car. The companion, believed to have been John Hamilton, was hit and dropped his gun. Dillinger helped him into the car, a blue Plymouth, and it roared away with bullets chasing it. Two game wardens who just happened to be passing joined in the turkey shoot, but the car disappeared toward the south. It was found abandoned next day full of bullet holes and blood stains, but of the men and the money there was no trace.

Five days later Dillinger and Evelyn reached Tucson. Other members of the gang had gotten there earlier, traveling separately with their girls.

But their stay had not been without incident.

Two of the boys had registered at the Congress Hotel. When it caught fire on January 22, 1934, they paid a fireman $50 to bring out their luggage. In those Depression days such a sum was large enough to arouse interest. The fireman thought about it for a day or two and then recognized pictures of the men in a magazine article devoted to the exploits of Dillinger's gang. By the time he passed on the tip to police, the men had moved to a house on North Second Avenue. One of Dillinger's aides was picked up quietly while pricing a radio in a downtown store. The other, nabbed at the rented house, put up a fight with some assistance from his girl, but succeeded only in breaking the finger of one of the arresting officers.

Delighted, the police kept the arrests quiet and staked out the house on Second Avenue. A few hours later a Terraplane—Dillinger's favorite automobile—pulled up in front of the house.

An object-lesson editorial cartoon that appeared after Dillinger's death.

John Dillinger at Crown Point jail with his captor, 5'3" Sheriff Lillian Holley. This photo, with its feeling of comraderie, caused a furor in the press and law enforcement agencies. *Opposite page*, Dillinger holds in his left hand the whittled gun he used for his escape.

SLAYER'S BOLD ESCAPE IS MADE WITH TOY GUN

Ease of Desperado's Flight Arouses Comment.

Locks Up Deputies and Flees in Sheriff's Car.

How it was possible for John Dillinger to outwit a dozen or more guards hired especially to watch him and then walk leisurely from the supposedly escape-proof Crown Point jail was a subject of discussion among public officials and citizens generally in Chicago and other cities last night.

Indiana authorities seemed bewildered by the getaway. Chicago police officials said they were "disgusted." Other commentators accused Sherif Lillian Holley and Prosecuting Attorney Robert G. Estill of Lake county f being too lenient with the prisner.

Judge Blochs Removal.

That an effort had been made take the prisoner to the state nitentiary at Michigan City for afekeeping pending his trial was disclosed last night by Judge William J. Murray of the Lake county Circuit court. Judge Murray said that he had presumed the prisoner's removal and the responsibility on his shoulders for his act.

Prosecutor Estill came to-day with an application for Dillinger's transfer from the jail to the peni-

Pictures of the career of John Dillinger and his desperadoes are on page 15. Map and photos showing how escape was effected are on page 19.

Several thousand policemen Illinois, Indiana, and Ohio last night were conducting a widespread hunt for John Dillinger one time Indiana farm boy who grew into the nation's most notorious killer and bank robber.

Dillinger, aided only by his own desperate courage and a little toy pistol he had made himself escaped yesterday morning from the heavily guarded jail at Crown Point.

is Herbert Youngblood of Ga Negro, who was awaiting trial f murder and welcomed the opportunity to flee. Both are ful armed, having taken two machine guns and a number of pisto from the jail arsenal.

It is the belief of the authorities that Dillinger, at least, will hate to shoot if cornered.

Identity of Fugitives.

The fugitives taken by this r man, who fled in a seized autom in their escape. There w

The car had Wisconsin license plates and it contained a man and a woman. The man opened the door, got out slowly, and glanced around. From all sides, the police closed in. Dillinger, for by now there was no question, turned back suddenly. The officers drew their guns.

"I'm at the wrong house," said Dillinger.

The police disagreed. Searching their prisoner they found an automatic in a shoulder holster and $8,000 in cash. Part of the money was traced to that bank in East Chicago. More money and a small arsenal was found in the house. Bond was set at $100,000, and lawmen from around the nation flocked to Tucson to identify Dillinger and claim the right to try him in their jurisdiction. The press had a gala and a lot of statements were attributed to Dillinger that must have been news to him.

Quite a battle developed between the Wisconsin and Indiana delegations. Dillinger favored the Wisconsin group and waived extradition to that state, but Arizona officials gave the nod to Indiana on the grounds that Wisconsin had no death penalty for capital crimes. It was necessary to drag Dillinger from his cell when Indiana officials tried to take custody. The stewardess on the plane back to Indiana told reporters on arrival that she felt sorry for Dillinger. He looked like "a little puppy with his tail between his legs," she added.

A small army met the plane in Chicago and convoyed Dillinger to the Lake County Jail at Crown Point, Indiana. The local newspaper noted he arrived with "an escort of police, deputy sheriffs, special detectives armed with machine guns, rifles, revolvers, sawed-off shotguns, bulletproof armor and bulletproof vests such as was never seen before at one time in the middle west."

And Dillinger was turned over to a five-foot, three-inch woman—Sheriff Lillian Holley—who had been named to succeed her late husband after he had been killed in a fight with a mentally-disturbed citizen.

A month went by. Fears that Dillinger's gang would assault the jail and free their leader slowly ebbed. Plans moved ahead to try the prisoner for the killing of Officer O'Malley. Meanwhile, Dillinger sat in a cell with three other felons. Someone sent him a Bible but he preferred to play cards with his cellmates or to whittle. Why he was allowed a knife is one of those puzzles never explained. That he was skilled in its use became apparent as he carved out tops that were balanced enough to

DAILY TRIBUNE

CONVICT IN CAB HOLDS UP GUARD AND DRIVES AWAY

Gets Gun After Trial and Second Conviction.

George [Baby Face] Nelson, 23 years old, bank bandit and convict, overpowered his guard and escaped last night just outside the prison walls in Joliet. The young convict was being retur... prison...

Nelson's Crime Career Began as Auto Thief

"He's a clever kid!"

That was how the family of George [Baby Face] Nelson, 27 years old, now America's No. 1 public enemy, received the news yesterday that Nelson...

NOVEMBER 28, 1934

'CLEVER KID,' SISTER OF NELSON CALLS HIM

"If They Get Him They'll Be Taking Him to Morgue, Not to a Cell."

Special to the Post-Dispatch.

CHICAGO, Nov. 28.—Lester M. Gillis, 27 years old, is "a clever kid." That is what his sister thinks of the man known as George (Baby...

"Baby Face" Nelson at age three, when he really could be called "Baby Face."

spin, propellers which revolved when blown upon, and little boats that certainly would have sailed had there been water on which to launch them. He showed the toys to guards and visitors alike, displaying a rather naive pride in his creations. Soon the sight of "the whittler" at work became so commonplace as not to rate a second look.

On March 3, 1934, Dillinger made his move. Action began in the exercise bullpen on the second floor. A turnkey who had served several terms for drunkenness appeared, and Dillinger thrust what the man thought was a pistol into his side. He forced the elderly man to call the warden, then various deputies. Each was locked up in turn, but since none were permitted to carry guns inside the jail Dillinger was still armed with his original weapon. Herbert Youngblood, an accused murderer, accepted Dillinger's invitation to join the jail break; and with one man as hostage they walked out of the cellblock and into the receiving room. There Dillinger collected an automatic, a submachine gun, and two new prisoners. He escorted the prisoners back to the cells where the others were locked up, and deposited them. It was then he dropped his bomb:

"I did it all with my little wooden gun," he said.

The gun, whittled out carefully, had been darkened with shoe polish and then embellished with parts of a safety razor.

Still laughing he went down to the basement with Youngblood and Ernest Blunk, a fingerprint expert serving as hostage. None of the cars in the basement would start. Unabashed, Dillinger went outside the building and around to the main garage.

"Which is the fastest car?" he asked.

Edwin Saager, the head mechanic, thought Dillinger was a special deputy. Strangers wandering around with submachine gus had become commonplace. Without hesitation he indicated the sheriff's car, a black V-8 parked near the door.

"Let's take it," said Dillinger.

He ordered Blunk to drive and got in the seat beside him. Youngblood forced Saager into the rear seat. Blunk did his best to attract attention, almost hitting a car as he pulled out of the garage and running red lights. But no one noticed anything. As they passed the bank Dillinger said he was tempted to stop and rob it. He told Blunk to slow down and began whistling the refrain of "I'm heading for the last roundup." Eventually the car skidded into a ditch. It took thirty minutes to get it out, but Dillinger seemed unconcerned. A few miles down the road he

George "Baby Face" Nelson.

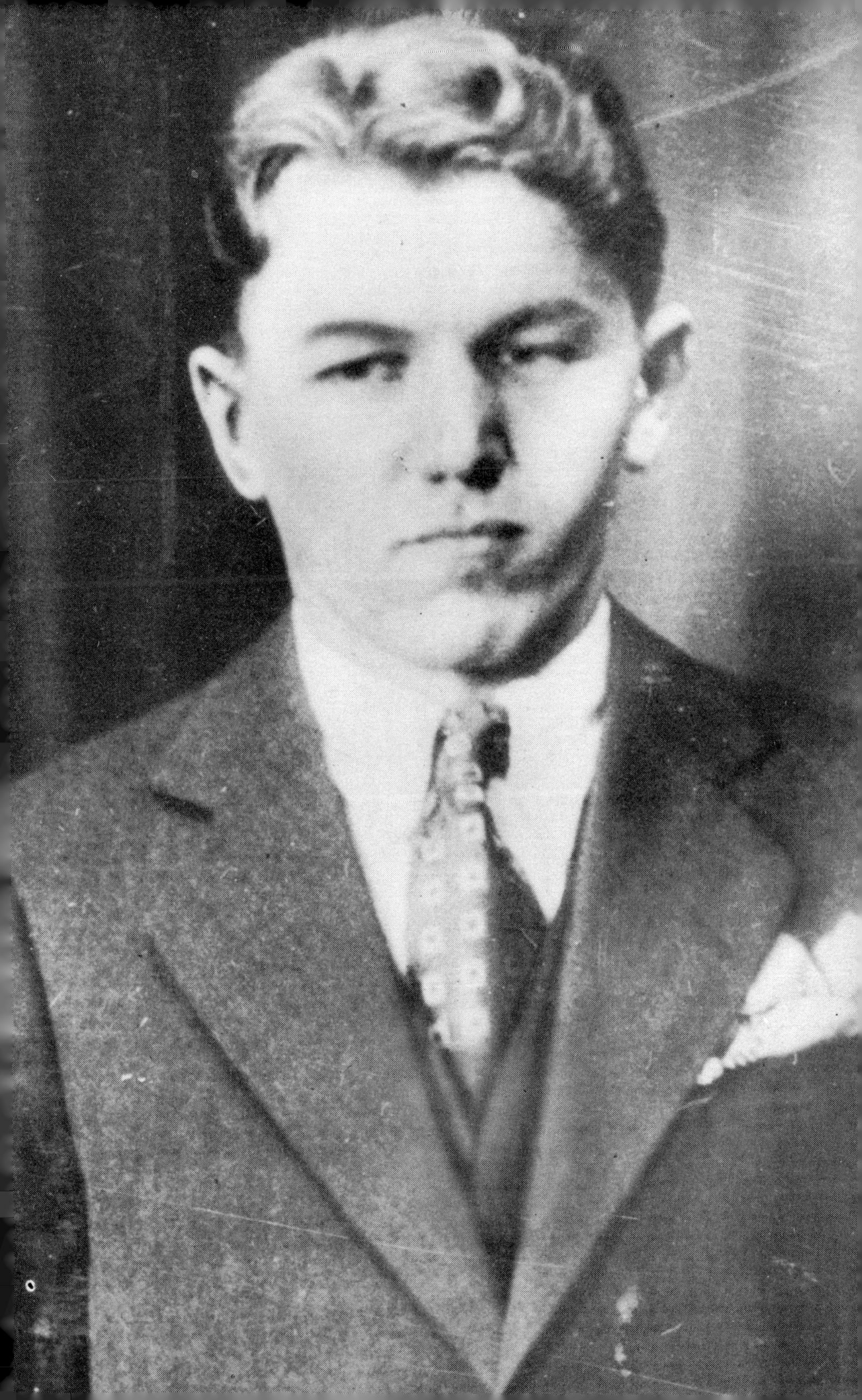

Scene of Dillinger's Escape, Resort Window Shattered By Gunfire, and Federal Agent Who Was Killed

Top, Little Bohemia Lodge, the roadhouse near Mercer, Wisconsin, where FBI agent W. Carter Baum (*bottom left*) was killed by "Baby Face" Nelson.

released the two prisoners, giving them $4 for carfare of the $15 he had taken from the deputies back at the jail. His performance throughout won Saager's admiration. "He seemed like an honest fellow," Saager was quoted as saying.

The sheriff's car was found abandoned on the streets of Chicago, a fact that enabled the FBI to officially enter the case under the Dyer Act which prohibited the interstate transportation of stolen vehicles. Meanwhile, the jail at Lima, Ohio, where three of Dillinger's gang were awaiting trial, was ringed with barbed wire and sandbags. National Guardsmen manned machine guns. Searchlights played on the battlements at night and a brigadier general was in command. Various nervous individuals reported "seeing" Dillinger in the vicinity, and reports circulated that the bandit had dressed seven men in stolen National Guard uniforms and planned to march them in and take over. After the wooden gun episode anything seemed possible.

While the excitement raged, Dillinger and Evelyn slipped into St. Paul, Minnesota, a town firmly controlled by politicians in the pay of the Kid Cann Gang. There he quickly recruited some allies, the most famous of which was Lester Gillis—the infamous Baby Face Nelson of crime mythology. Just three days after his escape from Crown Point, the revitalized Dillinger Gang robbed the Security National Bank at Sioux Falls, South Dakota, of $46,000. It was a typical production, complete with hostages and a chase. The escape car broke down with the pursuers within gun shot, but the outlaws fired a few bursts with their submachine guns, commandeered a farmer's car, and rode happily away unmolested.

One week later the gang struck again. The target was the Mason City, Iowa, bank. The loot was $52,000. Dillinger was wounded, the shot coming from an office above the bank. They headed back to St. Paul where the city health officer treated the wound and said nothing about it until much later. Dillinger then collected another wound a few days later when trapped momentarily by FBI agents in an apartment in St. Paul. A puzzled landlord had tipped the agents after noting that his tenants always left the building by the rear door. Of such details was the FBI's reputation for detective work constructed.

Five days after the narrow escape Dillinger attended a family reunion on his father's farm at Mooresville, Indiana. His older sister baked coconut cream pies and fried chicken, and the entire tribe ate its fill. The guest of honor posed for pictures,

Above, the scene of W. Carter Baum's killing, the road leading to Little Bohemia Lodge. Another FBI agent and a constable were wounded during their escape in the officer's car. *Right and opposite page*, Nelson arrest pictures.

holding the famous wooden gun in one hand and a submachine gun in the other. An hour after he left the farm the FBI moved into a vacant house down the road. From then on the Dillinger home was under observation. When reporters learned of the reunion they flocked to the farm. The elder Dillinger confirmed it and added:

"I didn't tell the police because they didn't ask me."

But things weren't going too well for Dillinger despite the fun and games. One day after the visit home he had an appointment in a tavern in Chicago. Evelyn was with him as he approached, and she suggested that perhaps she'd better go in first and case the joint. The FBI was waiting. Dillinger circled the block once and didn't stop when Evelyn failed to reappear. Later he stopped long enough to telephone an attorney and ask him to represent his girl, who was being grilled for hours in an effort to learn Dillinger's plans. She didn't reveal any.

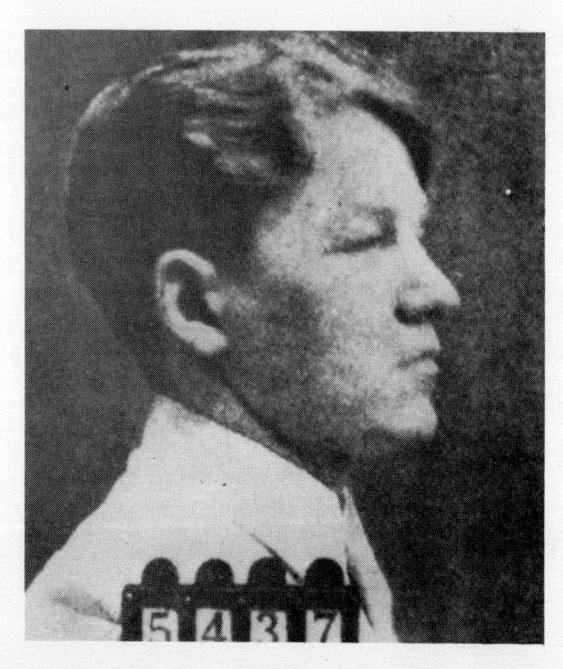

The outlaw, who was now a legend in his own time, surfaced again in Warsaw, Indiana, long enough to rob the jail of some weapons. And in Mooresville some citizens drew up a petition and sent it to the governor. It recalled the fact that Frank James had been permitted to surrender and live out his life in peace, and it suggested that Dillinger should be granted the same privilege. The elder Dillinger, who was becoming a celebrity, allowed that it was a good idea. He thought his son might make a good policeman. Governor McNutt didn't agree. Then the same people who signed the first petition circulated another one asking that a company of National Guardsmen be stationed in Mooresville for protection. McNutt was equally unresponsive. The good citizens of Dillinger's hometown apparently believed there was safety in ambiguity.

The scene quickly shifted to an isolated roadhouse in the wilds of Wisconsin. On Friday, April 20, 1934, the proprietor, Emil Wanatka, was delighted to see a car come in containing two men and a woman. Later in the afternoon two more cars arrived, bringing the guest total to six men and four women. Among those present were Dillinger and Baby Face Nelson, but it was Saturday before the host recognized his famous visitor. Dillinger assured him there was nothing to worry about, he said later. He seemed supremely confident and raised no objections when Mrs. Wanatka asked permission to attend a cousin's birthday party. Once away from Little Bohemia, as the roadhouse was called, she hunted up her brother-in-law and gave him the news. Next morning the brother-in-law drove sixty miles to find a safe telephone and called Melvin Purvis at the FBI office in Chicago.

John Edgar Hoover was consulted in Washington and soon every special agent in several states was rushing toward Little Bohemia by land and air. By Sunday evening a number of men had reached Rhinelander, two hours away by car. They arrived none too soon for Dillinger announced abruptly that his party was leaving that evening instead of the following day as he had originally intended to do. Somehow the word was conveyed to Purvis, giving him no choice but to attack as quickly as possible. Meanwhile, Wanatka offered his guests Sunday dinner. Among the extra guests were some men from a nearby Civilian Conservation Corps camp who had just dropped in for a change of menu.

Dinner over, the CCC men got in their car and started to leave. All hell broke loose. The FBI men had just arrived and, taking no chances, opened up with submachine guns when they saw three unidentified men leaving so abruptly. One man was killed instantly and the other two were wounded.

The moment the shooting started, Dillinger and his male companions ran out the back door and into the woods. The

Above, three members of Dillinger's gang, including Harry Pierpont, are escorted to the Ohio State Penitentiary after their conviction for murder of a sheriff. They are covered front and rear by machine guns. The entourage of soldiers, police, and county officials take no chances, perhaps inhibited by the Kansas City massacre of a few months before. *Left*, J. Edgar Hoover.

Bystanders grouped around the bloodied pavement where Dillinger was gunned down.

Chicago D

THE WORLD'S G

CENTS PAY NO MORE!

F. XCIII.—NO. 175 C.   MONDAY, JULY 23.

ILL DILLI

| VIOLENCE REATENED | NEWS SUMMARY | 14 ARE KILLED IN BUS CRASH; | TH |

ily **Tribune** | FINA

EST NEWSPAPER

—28 PAGES · PRICE TWO CENTS

IGER HER

ADY OF THE LAKE | SLAIN BY U. S. AGEN

AS HE LEAVES THEAT

women took shelter in the basement. Purvis in his haste had not had time to surround the lodge or to establish roadblocks. Dillinger and two men walked a mile to another resort where they forced a native to drive them away in his car. Around midnight they let their driver go and gave him seven dollars to get home on.

Baby Face Nelson, meanwhile, reached Birchwood Lodge and was in the process of taking a car when up drove an FBI agent and two constables. Before they could pull their guns, Nelson cut loose with a makeshift submachine pistol. The special agent was killed and the constables wounded. Nelson made good his flight as did the other members of the gang.

A shocked Purvis refused to believe his quarry had escaped. All through the night the siege continued. In Washington, FBI Director Hoover formally announced to the waiting world that Dillinger was cornered. The special agents poured volleys into the lodge, undiscouraged by the absence of return fire. And as dawn broke they filled the building with tear gas and waited, hands on triggers, for the inevitable climax.

Out marched three tearful women, their hands in the air.

It was the biggest fiasco since the raid on Jesse James's home.

Apologetically, the FBI announced the men had broken through the cordon and vanished.

Three months passed before Dillinger surfaced again. The heat was on as publicity—the ultimate weapon—made his name and face known throughout the midwest in particular and the country in general. The FBI sorted through thousands of false leads, confident that in the end there would be one that would prove out. And one would be enough.

Aware of the danger, Dillinger tried to change his appearance and his fingerprints. Plastic surgery was performed with no great success, and his fingertips were seared with acid. But Dillinger made no move to get out of the country. He was, after all, something of a provincial who liked familiar scenes and faces.

He also like women—and perhaps trusted them too much. Hiding out in Chicago, he got lonesome for Evelyn who was awaiting trial on charges of harboring a fugitive. Since she wasn't available the obvious solution was to find a substitute. He asked a cab driver and was directed to the home of Mrs. Anna Sage, a former madam in Gary, Indiana, who now operated a call-girl service.

A still from the last film Dillinger ever saw, *Manhattan Melodrama*, with Myrna Loy and Clark Gable.

Mrs. Sage, who recognized an opportunity when she recognized Dillinger, was eager to cooperate. She offered the well-heeled customer a room in her apartment and she called over Polly Keele, a blue-eyed, diminutive redhead. Polly was the ex-wife of a Gary policeman. She liked Dillinger instantly. In fact, she insisted she was "crazy" about him. And Dillinger responded with one of his typical quick passions. Always happy to help the cause of romance was Mrs. Sage. She suggested Polly move into the apartment and share Dillinger's room. Polly thought it a great idea.

While John and Polly made love, attended baseball games, and caught as many movies as possible, Mrs. Sage was busy with business of her own. She was facing deportation to her native Romania and the prospect was unappealing. Learning that Martin Zarovich had been assigned to the case, she contacted him. Zarovich was an East Chicago policeman who had been a buddy of the slain cop, William O'Malley, and a friend of Mrs. Sage when she was operating a brothel at Gary. Zarovich arranged for the woman to meet Special Agent Melvin Purvis and after some discussion a deal was made. Purvis agreed to ask the Justice Department to intervene in her deportation case and Mrs. Sage agreed to deliver Dillinger.

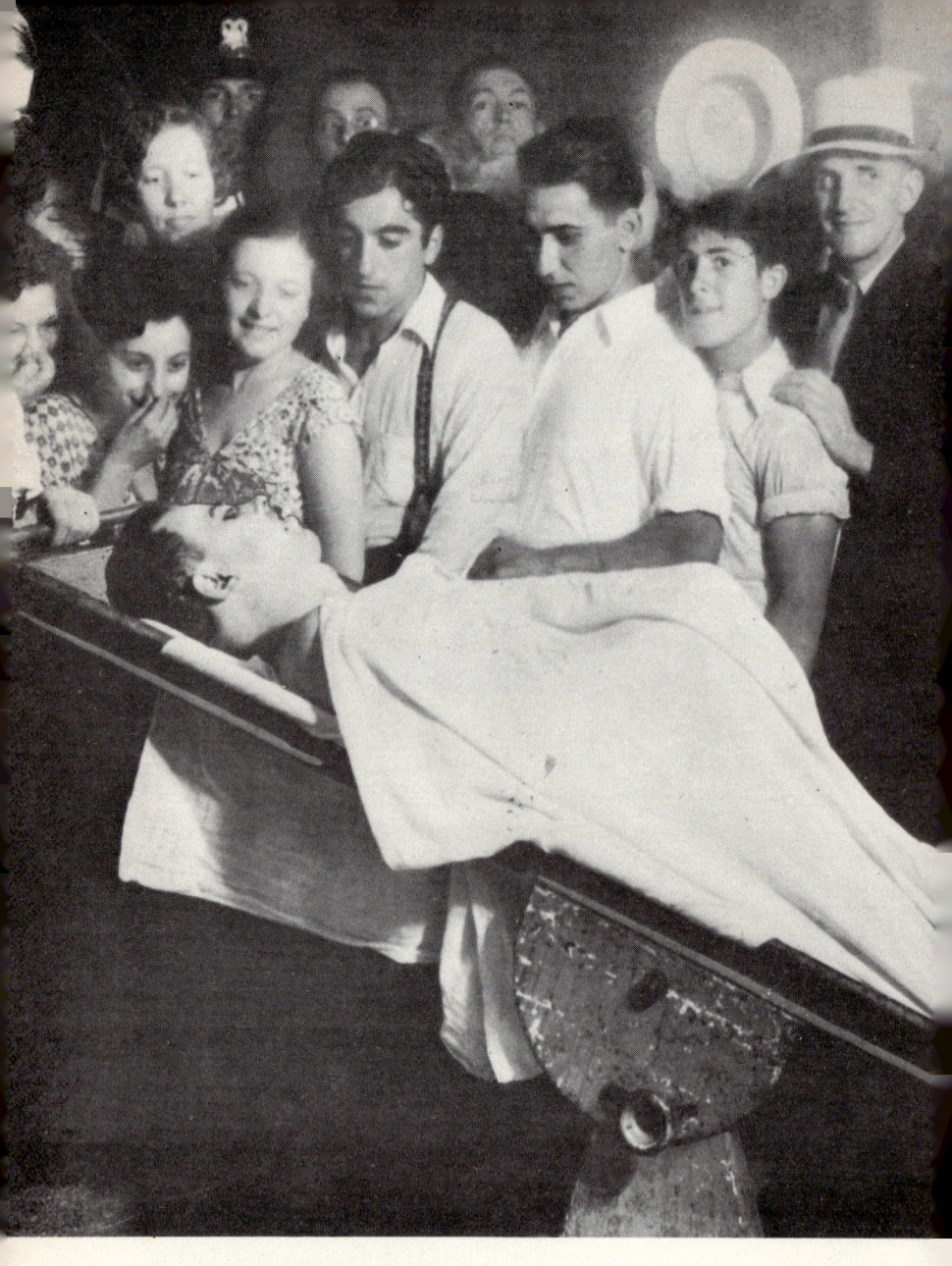

Coroner Frank J. Walsh stands at Dillinger's head as a long line of people pass in front of a glass panel to view the body as it lies on a slab. Note the women holding their noses, probably due to the stench of formaldehyde. The undertaker was refused the body until the curious had had their fill.

THRONGS FIGHT FOR GLIMPSE OF DEAD DILLINGER

Undertaker Refused Body Till Curious Got Fill.

BY VIRGINIA GARDNER.

The Cook county morgue at Polk and Wood streets was a lively spot yesterday and last evening as crowds of spectators jammed in to get a view of the body of John Dillinger. For sev-

CROWD STORMS MORGUE TO SEE OUTLAW'S BODY

Reveal Dillinger Seared Fingers in Acid.

"There he is!"

These words were whispered in awed tones early this morning by a young woman, not more than 19 years of age, as she, with a dozen other persons, pressed her face against a ground level meshed window of the county morgue. All were gazing in fascination upon a busy group in the center of a large basement room.

The curious crowd at the window was typical. At every available window and door crushed groups of men and women who hoped to get a glimpse of America's most notorious outlaw—dead. Inside the room were

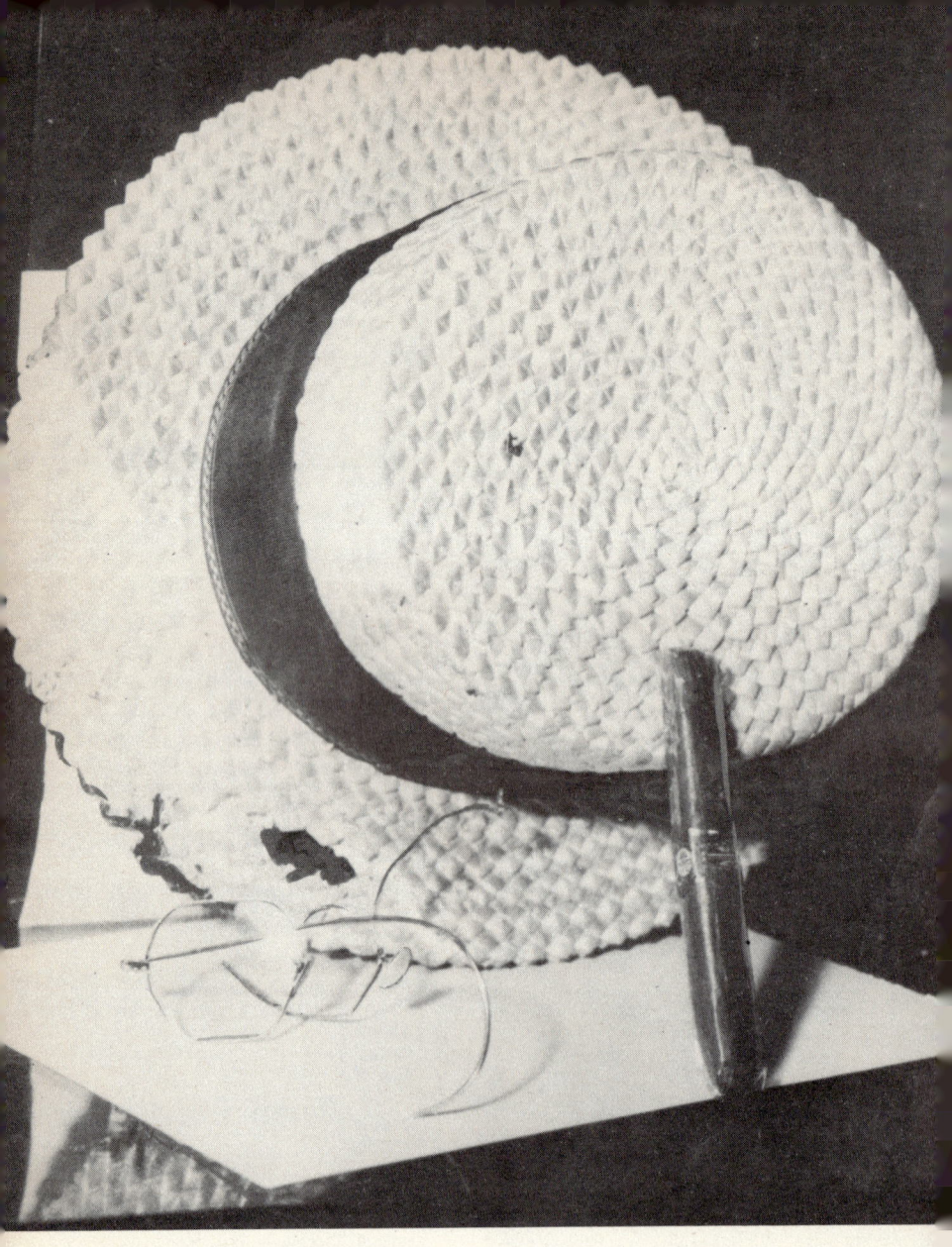

Dillinger's hat with bullet hole, his shattered glasses, and a cigar—some of his last effects.

On July 22, 1934, the end came. Dillinger escorted his mistress and his madam to the Biograph Theater on North Lincoln Avenue to see Clark Gable in *Manhattan Melodrama*— a typical gangster movie in which the handsome hood won everyone's heart before coming to the bad end demanded by the Hay's Office. Purvis and sixteen special agents were waiting. A telephone line to Hoover in Washington was kept open so the director could be the first to hear—and break—the news. Mrs. Sage wore an orange-colored skirt as a signal that the Biograph was the theater selected. Subsequently reporters, acting on crumbs of information, changed the color and turned "the lady in red" into Dillinger's sweetheart.

No move was made when the party entered the theater. Dillinger would be allowed to enjoy one more movie. But when he came out, the special agents closed in. Mrs. Sage lagged behind. Sensing trouble, Dillinger turned. Allegedly he made a motion to draw a gun. Four bullets struck Dillinger. He fell forward on his face, dead before he hit the concrete. The women ran.

Anna Sage was given $5,000, and removed to San Francisco, allegedly for her protection. Eventually she was deported to Romania—again for her protection. She died there in 1947.

Purvis, who had made the deal with her, resigned from the FBI a year later to cash in on his fame. He wrote a book and allowed his name to be used by Post Toasties as head of the "Junior G-Men" which handed out badges in return for box tops. He killed himself in 1960.

The elder Dillinger followed Frank James's example and became a lecturer with a traveling carnival. His topic: "Crime Doesn't Pay." Evelyn, released from prison, joined the show as John Dillinger's girlfriend.

Dillinger was buried at Crown Hill Cemetery near Indianapolis amid scenes of great excitement. A slab of concrete was poured above the coffin to protect the body from souvenir seekers.

In FBI headquarters in Washington a "death mask" of Dillinger remained on display for thirty-eight years and was removed only after the death of Hoover in 1972.

Next to Hoover, perhaps, John H. Dillinger was the man most responsible for the FBI legend. And maybe, just maybe, that was enough to let him join his mother in heaven as had been his ambition in Sunday School.

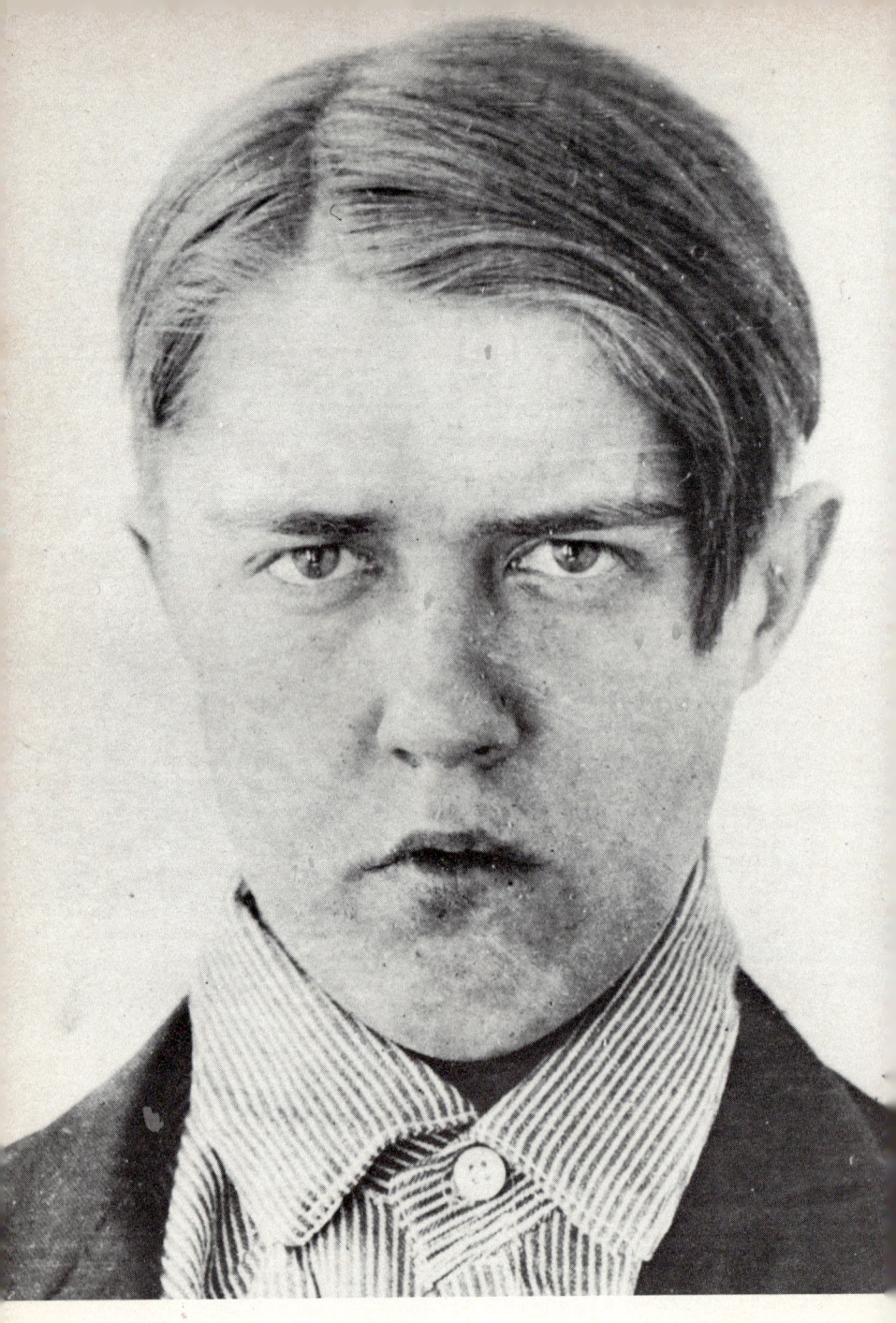

Alvin Karpis as a boy burglar, age sixteen, when he was sentenced to the Kansas reformatory.

5
Old Creepy was a Thief

LEGEND HAS A habit of ignoring facts it finds nonmalleable as witness Albin Karpowitz, a citizen of Canada.

John Edgar Hoover called him "Rat." His associates in the U.S. underworld spoke fondly of him as "Old Creepy." He became infamous as Alvin Karpis.

Born in Montreal in 1908 to Lithuanian parents, brought to Topeka, Kansas, as a boy, Karpis was indeed rootless. His father, a hardworking farmer-artist, assumed his son would hustle as he did to make an honest living. The idea doesn't seem to have occurred to Karpis—as a conscious thought, anyway. He found it too easy to pick up a dishonest dollar running errands for gamblers and whores who operated freely in the vicinity. Those respectable citizens who treat juvenile delinquency as a problem separate and apart from adult delinquency might well ponder the circumstances that made Karpis a natural criminal. Vice may not be so serious as armed robbery, perhaps, but it breeds disrespect for *all* laws in youths growing up in a so-called "wide-open" community.

By age ten Karpis was ready to move up into what he considered the "big leagues." With a reform-school graduate as his guide, he became a burglar. In the next five years he took what he pleased, his confidence growing with each successful job. It was small stuff, but it satisfied his needs and his ego at that point in his development. By age seventeen he was operating a hamburger joint that served as a front for bootleg liquor and warehouse robbery. Like Richard M. Nixon he was fascinated by train whistles in the night. Unlike Nixon, however, he acted on that interest and began riding the rails and seeing the country. Logically, he also began dreaming of the day he would be a train robber.

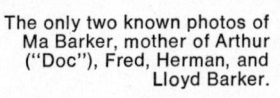

The only two known photos of Ma Barker, mother of Arthur ("Doc"), Fred, Herman, and Lloyd Barker.

The first brush with the forces of law and order came when he was picked up in Florida for vagrancy—picked up on the roof of a train—and sentenced to thirty days on the chain gang. That was an adventure. A year later when he was caught in a warehouse and sentenced to five years—that was an education.

After three years, he decided he was ready to graduate. His principal tutor agreed and the pair broke out of prison and began a grand tour of the West—stealing everything they needed from cars to clothes as they went. His friend got picked up and sent back to prison. By working overtime in the coal mine at the Kansas prison, he got his sentence reduced and rejoined Karpis. But he got out this time with a cause. His friends back there needed new clothes, he said. They were permitted to wear their own clothes, so long as they had some, but many had no way to replenish their wardrobes. Obviously, the poor guys needed help. Karpis agreed. The daring duo broke into a haberdashery in Bristow, Oklahoma, and spent a Sunday night picking out clothes for their friends. The outfits were mailed in separate boxes to the prison and—as they later discovered—were routinely delivered. It was one way to make friends and influence prisoners.

The Depression was heavy on the land and the business of robbery was suffering. There just wasn't much money in circulation. Any self-respecting robber had to keep working just to make ends meet. That requirement greatly increased the odds, and in March, 1930, Karpis and his pal were picked up on suspicion. In those not-so-innocent days, little attention was paid to a suspect's civil rights. Perhaps, as hard-liners insist, that made it easy to get evidence. If so, there is nothing on record to suggest that the crime rate was decreased one whit. Moreover, the absence of strict procedures encouraged corruption on a large scale. Certainly, any historian would have to agree that at a time when the third degree was a standard technique, there was unprecedented lawlessness and widespread corruption. A lot of Americans, unemployed and bitter, had turned to unrestrained free enterprise instead of revolution.

Karpis was beaten for three days before finally admitting he was an escaped convict. The police were disappointed—they had hoped to pin a lot of unsolved burglaries on him and thus improve their record. He got himself transferred to Lansing, where he had a lot of well-dressed friends, and used the coal piles as a shortcut to freedom. Before getting out, however, he met and became friends with Freddie Barker. And lo—the Karpis-Barker Gang of FBI legend was born. A hillbilly from the Ozarks, Freddie knew how to live. He was well supplied with canned foods, books, and marijuana. The latter was cultivated on a prison farm on an island in the Missouri River, and sold for twenty-five cents a tobacco can.

It was all a lot of fun, the youthful Karpis decided.

Before proceeding with the fun and games, however, it would be best to consider the question of Ma Barker, the mother of Karpis's new friend. Here is how FBI Director Hoover saw her or, more accurately, sought to have the country see her:

"Crime annals knew her as the most vicious, dangerous and resourceful criminal brain of the last decade. . . . In her sixty or so years, this woman became a monument to the evils of parental indulgence. Of her four sons, one became a mail robber, another a holdup man, and the remaining pair were highwaymen, kidnappers, wanton murderers. To a great extent, their criminal careers were directly traceable to their mother; to her they looked for guidance, for daring resourcefulness. . . . She kept open house for big-time criminality. With the calm of a person ordering a meal she brought about bank robberies, holdups or kidnappings and commanded the slayings of persons who, only a short time before, had enjoyed what they thought was her friendship. . . ."

Quite an indictment by Mr. Hoover, And it, perhaps, tells as much about Hoover as it does about Ma Barker. Consider the charge that she was "the most vicious, dangerous and resourceful brain of the last decade." This rating puts her ahead of such men as Louis (Lepke) Buchalter, alleged head of Murder, Inc. It puts her above Meyer Lansky, now known as the financial wizard of organized crime. And so on. Obviously, at the time Hoover made that statement in 1938 he knew very little about what was going on in the country.

But, ratings aside, are his charges against the old lady valid? Karpis says they are not. In his 1971 book, *The Alvin Karpis Story*, he noted:

Ma was none of these things. She wasn't a leader of criminals or even a criminal herself. The proof is that in her entire life she was never mugged or printed by the police. There is not one official police photograph of her in existence or a set of fingerprints taken while she was alive . . . . It's no insult to Ma's memory that she just didn't have the brains or know-how to direct us on a robbery.

Left, top and bottom, Arthur "Doc" Barker. *Right,* Fred Barker. These two had a career in crime dating from 1918 that included larceny, jail-breaking, bank robbery, kidnapping, and murder.

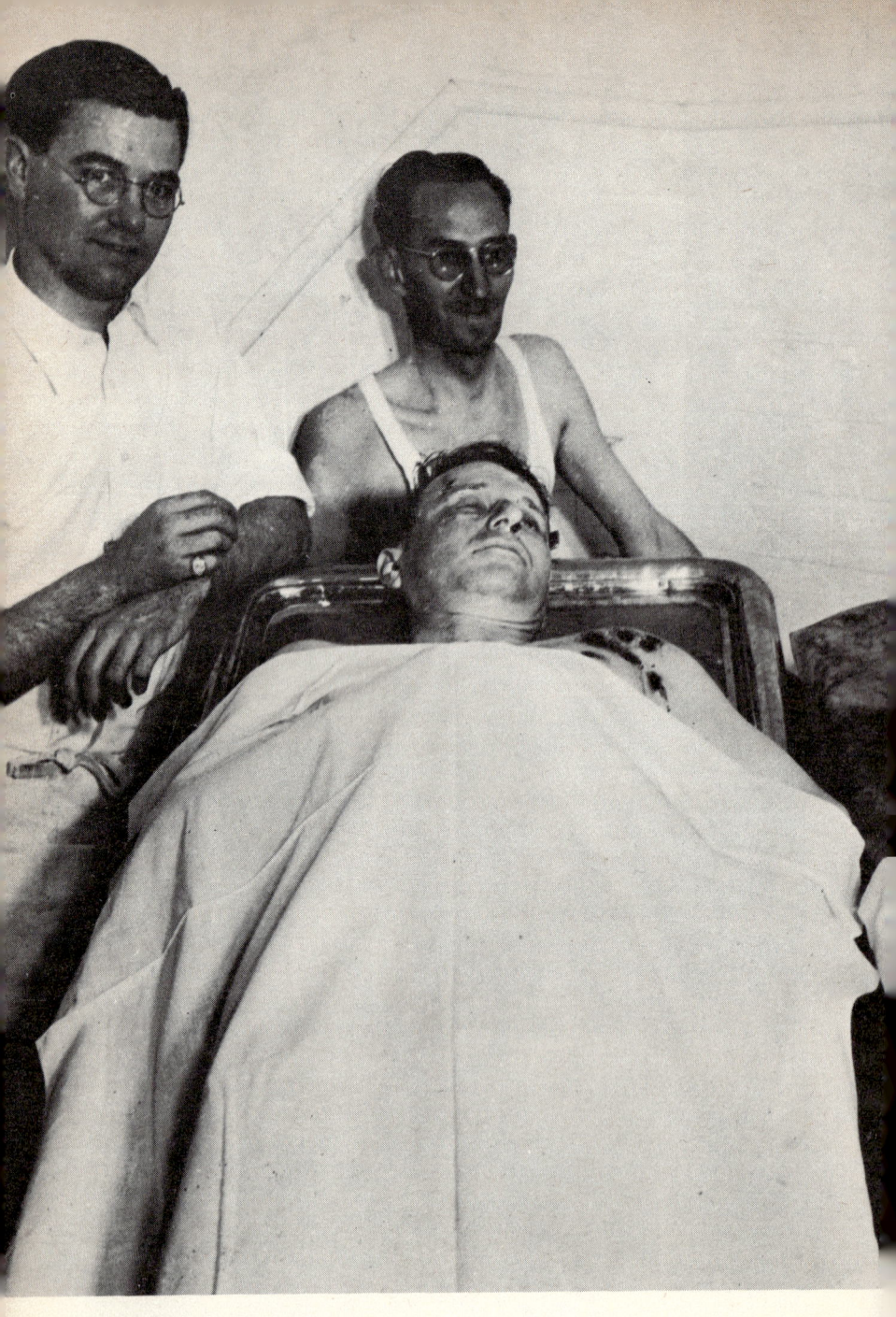

Fred Barker and his mother, Kate Barker, shown on slabs in the morgue at Ocala, Florida, after being killed by federal agents on January 16, 1935.

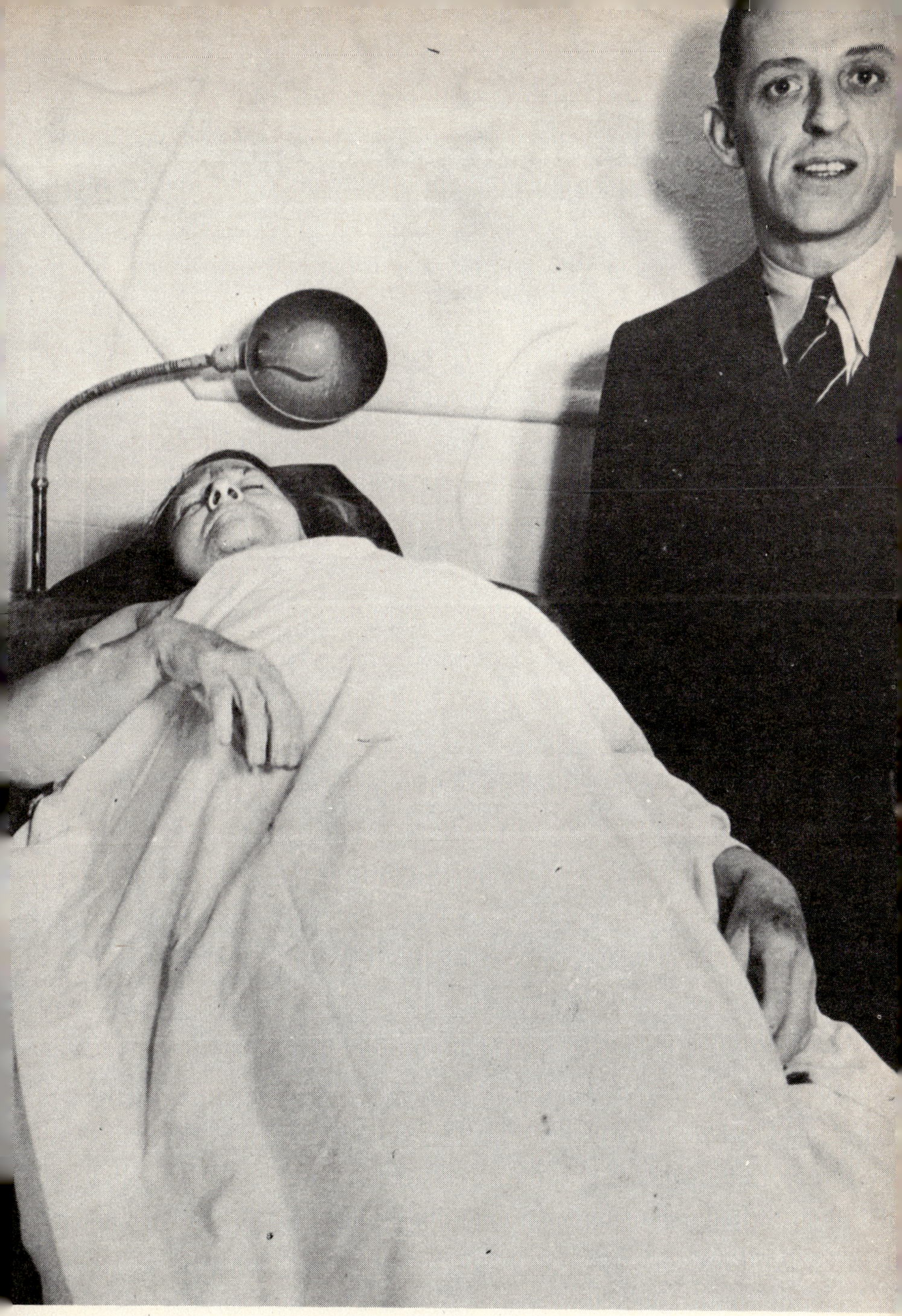

It wouldn't have occurred to her to get involved in our business, and we always made a point of only discussing our scores when Ma wasn't around . . . . She was just an old-fashioned homebody from the Ozarks . . . . Ma was superstitious gullible, simple, cantankerous and, well, generally law-abiding. She wasn't suited for a role in the Karpis-Barker Gang.

The key words in this defense insofar as the author—a hillbilly from the Blue Ridge—is concerned, are: "It wouldn't have occurred to her to get involved in our business." This rings true. Mountain people of that generation made a sharp distinction between men's business and women's business. It was man's business to run the still, fight the feuds, and generally provide for and protect his family. It was woman's business to cook, wash, and bind up the wounds of her men.

In short, the idea that a woman with Ma Barker's background could be a mastermind of crime, directing bank robberies and $300,000 kidnappings, is absurd on its face. Unwittingly, Hoover confirmed part of Karpis's defense brief when he stated:

"In all her life she was not once arrested. She was officially charged with only one crime, in spite of later revelations that she collaborated in them by the score. Barely able to read and write, she nevertheless knew every trick in the encyclopedia of criminality."

Gosh!

It was part of the code of the hills for sons to look after their mother. Hoover surely knew this, but his public view of all criminals as "rats" prevented him from acknowledging the Barker boys possesed decent instincts. But why build Ma up into a super-Rat? Karpis put it simply: "To justify the manner in which she met her death at the hands of the FBI."

If you're reluctant to take the word of an admitted crook, bear in mind the remarks of Assistant Attorney General Henry Petersen in 1973. Testifying at the Watergate hearings, Petersen commented on the problem of making the FBI admit it had ever been wrong.

Enough. We will leave "Bloody Mama" to the movies and proceed with the adventures of Karpowitz.

Karpis and Freddie Barker teamed up, forming the nucleus of the gang. Out of a larger group of approximately twenty trusted and experienced men, they selected two or three or five for the job at hand. The selection depended on who was

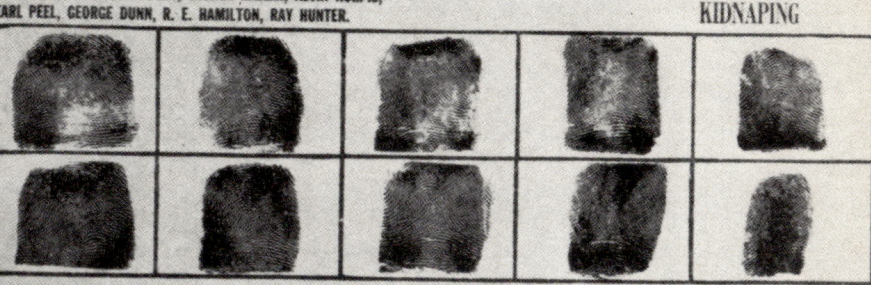

Alvin "Creepy" Karpis, Public Enemy Number One, in January, 1935, and his identification card.

available at that point in time, and the specific qualifications needed for each job. After the job was completed the gang broke up, usually into smaller groups, and then reassembled when a new challenge offered. Basically, however, each man considered himself independent, a free-lancer. He was under orders only during the planning and carrying out of a specific job. There was, however, a loose fraternity of crooks who helped each other in work and play when it could be done without imminent danger. When the chips were down, however, it was every man for himself. Both men and women understood this cruel code and accepted it. In many respects the friendships of men and their love affairs with women were similar to those developed by soldiers during a long war. One didn't become too close to a buddy who might be killed tomorrow, or to a girl who might be left alone for months or perhaps forever when luck abruptly ran out.

Loot was the avowed objective, but not really. Time and again Karpis and his pals drove out to take forbidding chances with money enough stashed away to enable them to live comfortably for years. No, as with most gangsters, there was much more involved. They liked their work. It was fun and it filled a need money alone could not.

Take the time Karpis, Freddie Barker, and another man looted the town of Cambridge, Minnesota. They arrived late at night, captured the only policeman on duty, and went up one street and down the other side—taking everything they wanted. To climax the caper, they stole a large touring car from the Buick agency and drove off in it.

Fun—but not really big-time stuff. Karpis was twenty-four when at last he took part in what he called "my first genuine major stickup." It was the Northwestern National Bank in Minneapolis and the year was 1932. Five men took part. The vault was cleaned out efficiently, and the men were about to depart when they noticed that squads of police had arrived and barricaded both ends of the street. Big deal. The robbers went out the back door where the car was parked and drove away without a shot being fired. The "take" was some $81,000 in cash and $185,000 in bonds. Fun, and profit, too.

Sometimes things got a bit grim, but that was all part of the fun. Like the time Freddie stopped the car and wandered up an alley to "take a leak."

Actually Freddie had borrowed Karpis's car to scout around

The arsenal taken from the Florida hideout of the Barkers after their shootout with federal officers.

the town of Pocahontas, Arkansas, and see if there was anything worth hitting. While he was taking a leak, a policeman wandered by and noticed the parked car. Strictly as a matter of routine he was jotting down the license number, when Freddie appeared out of the darkness and stuck his forty-five in the cop's back. He took the cop's gun and notebook and then took the cop for a ride to a gravel pit outside of town. As Freddie saw it, he had to choose between the car and the cop. That wasn't a hard choice. He shot the cop four times and left him dead.

Ordinarily, the murder would have bought some time, but kidneys were nervous in Pocahontas. The very next day a woman wandered off the road to take a leak and stumbled over the dead body. The heat went on, but not for long. A local citizen said he killed the cop, who turned out to be the night

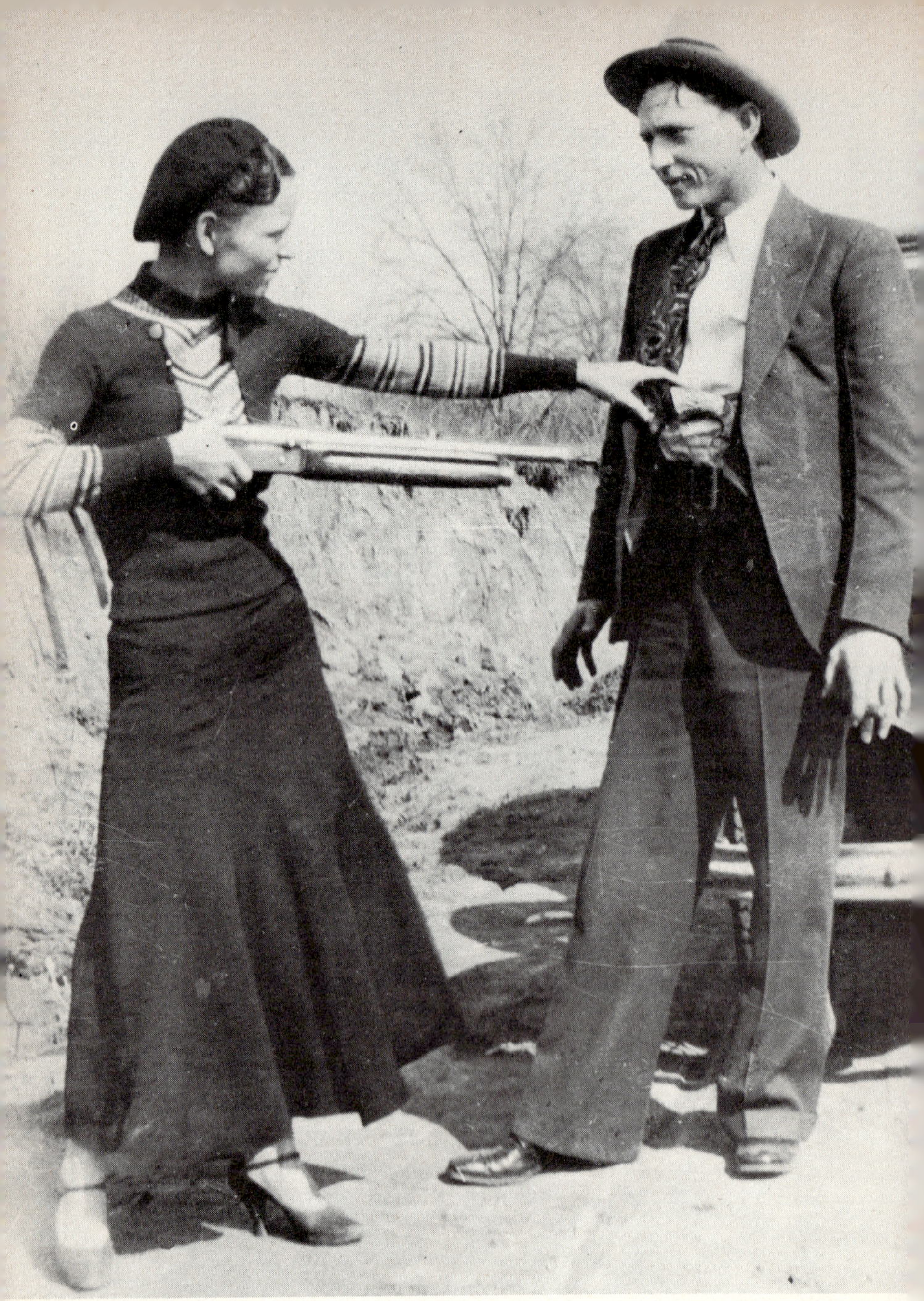

Opposite page, Bonnie Parker hamming it up for the camera with Clyde Barrow at the side of a road. *Left,* aside from cigars, she liked Bull Durham, while Clyde smoked Camel cigarettes.

BONNIE PARKER DIES BESIDE SWEETHEART RIDDLED WITH LEAD

TEXAS BAD MAN AND HIS GUN GIRL SLAIN BY POSSE

Drive Into Ambuscade at 85 Miles an Hour.

Clyde Barrow and Gangirl Shot Down by Texas Rangers and Louisiana Officers Near Arcadia

MAN-HUNTER SORRY WOMAN WAS KILLED

Trap Laid With Aid of Escaped Convict's Relative; Two Die With Weapons in Hands

(Pictures on back page.)

Gibsland, La., May 23.—[Special.]—Clyde Barrow, public enemy No. 1 of the southwest, and his cigar smoking gun moll, Bonnie Parker, died today with their boots on and guns in their hands. A posse of Texas rangers were in at the death.

The final act in the eight year

(By The Associated Press)

Arcadia, La., May 23.—Fifty bullets from the guns of old-time Texas Rangers and country sheriffs today ended the murderous career of Clyde Barrow and his blond gungirl woman, Bonnie Parker in an ambush laid in the woods of a graveled by-road south of here.

Acting on an underworld tip, the officers, led by the fearless manhunter, Frank Hamer, for 20 years a Texas Ranger, laid a trap for Barrow and his woman, who believed they were going to a rendezvous with an ex-convict associate.

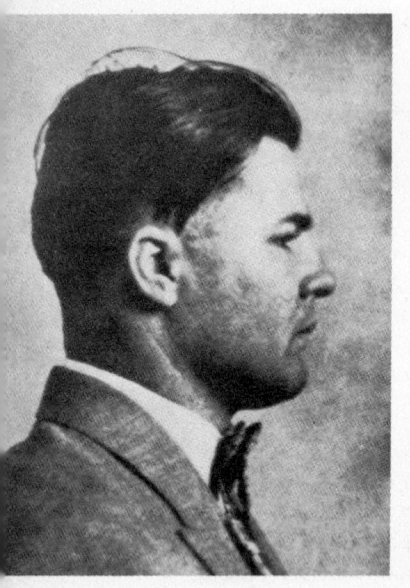

Top, Frank "Jelly" Nash, killed with four other men in an alleged attempt to rescue him at the Kansas City Massacre. *Bottom,* "Pretty Boy" Floyd, bank robber, murderer, associate of John Dillinger. He was killed by FBI agents in 1934.

chief, because the day chief persuaded him to do it. Freddie could take a leak in broad daylight after that.

Little towns were to rob. The big cities, controlled by syndicate gangsters, were places to relax, to hide out. They were safe. Cleveland was such a city, controlled as it was by the developing Cleveland Syndicate which over the next three decades would operate freely in Kentucky, West Virginia, Indiana, Florida, Nevada, and Cuba. Reno, which would eventually be supplanted by Las Vegas as "the biggest little city in the world," was another favorite. It was there that Karpis met Lester Gillis—the infamous Baby Face Nelson.

Nelson was hiding out in Reno under the protection of Jim McKay and Bill Graham, the men who fronted for the mob in legalizing gambling in Nevada. He had escaped from a train in Illinois where he was being moved under guard to stand trial on yet another charge of bank robbery. Karpis, who enjoyed having dinner with Baby Face and his family, promised to find employment for the bored killer. In 1933 he lined him up with John Dillinger.

After the bungled raid on Little Bohemia, in which Nelson killed an FBI agent while escaping, the heat was really on the youthful gunman. Following the death of Dillinger, the heat increased. Suddenly the "wise guys" in Reno, in Cleveland, and even in Chicago, where the friends of Al Capone still ruled, decided Baby Face was too hot to harbor. He crisscrossed the country, his faithful wife, Helen, always riding with him. In November, 1934, the end came. Two carloads of FBI agents engaged in a running duel with Nelson, his wife, and one companion-in-arms, John Paul Chase. Killed were Inspector Samuel Cowley and Special Agent Herman E. Hollis. Badly wounded, Nelson still managed to escape in the FBI's car—his own vehicle was too badly shot up to function. But it wasn't a victory to gloat about. Baby Face died that night in a nearby town. His blood-spattered body was found next morning when the sun rose. His wife had left it by a cemetery. An efficient woman was Helen Gillis. A good cook too, if Alvin Karpis is to be believed.

Nelson was not the only notorious character Karpis met in his wanderings. One day down in Joplin, Missouri, he was introduced to a couple who, to his way of thinking, looked like sharecroppers. They had blank faces, he recalled, like a lot of

Okies did in those dusty days, and their names were Clyde Barrow and Bonnie Parker.

Barrow was a cop killer and Bonnie was a nut. Together they created a lot of excitement in the Southwest. Barrow was believed to have killed fifteen people in his interstate travels, but it wasn't the FBI that brought him to an end. A Texas highway patrolman, formerly a member of the Texas Rangers, was responsible. Frank Hamer, a legend in his own right, started the hunt on February 10, 1934, and followed it for more than three months. Utilizing informers developed in a lifetime of police work, Hamer established a pattern of movement on the part of his quarry and so was waiting at a "post office" near Plain Dealing, Louisiana on the morning of May 23. Bonnie and Clyde drove up in a Ford sedan, stopped, and looked over at a stump where messages from his friends were hidden. Told to "stick 'em up" in the classic tradition, the couple grabbed their guns. Six men cut loose with automatic weapons and for Bonnie and Clyde the bloody honeymoon was over.

Karpis wasn't surprised to hear the news. He had not been impressed with the young couple.

Was Karpis an angel of doom in disguise? Shortly after meeting Bonnie and Clyde he teamed up with another man who didn't have long to live—Frank Nash. The job was a bank in Fairbury, Nebraska. Nash distinguished himself by jamming his submachine gun and in the midst of battle with an army of cops and vigilantes, Karpis had to stop and fix Nash's gun. It was a bloody shootout. One of the robbers was wounded and eight citizens, but no one died. The loot totaled almost $80,000 in cash and Liberty Bonds.

Nash was soon to figure in another shootout just as bloody—and a lot more fatal. Following the Fairbury robbery he went to Hot Springs, Arkansas, where, still celebrating, he got married to his girl, Frances, who deserved some sort of reward. Since Nash already had one wife, he conveniently adopted another name—George W. Miller—for his second bride.

Hot Springs didn't care. A "safe" town, a gambling town, it had been a hideout for hoods for decades and would so remain for decades. Owney "the Killer" Madden, an exiled gangster from New York City, had just moved to Hot Springs. Over the next thirty years he disciplined the town, eliminated the rowdy element, and built a gambling empire that endured until his death.

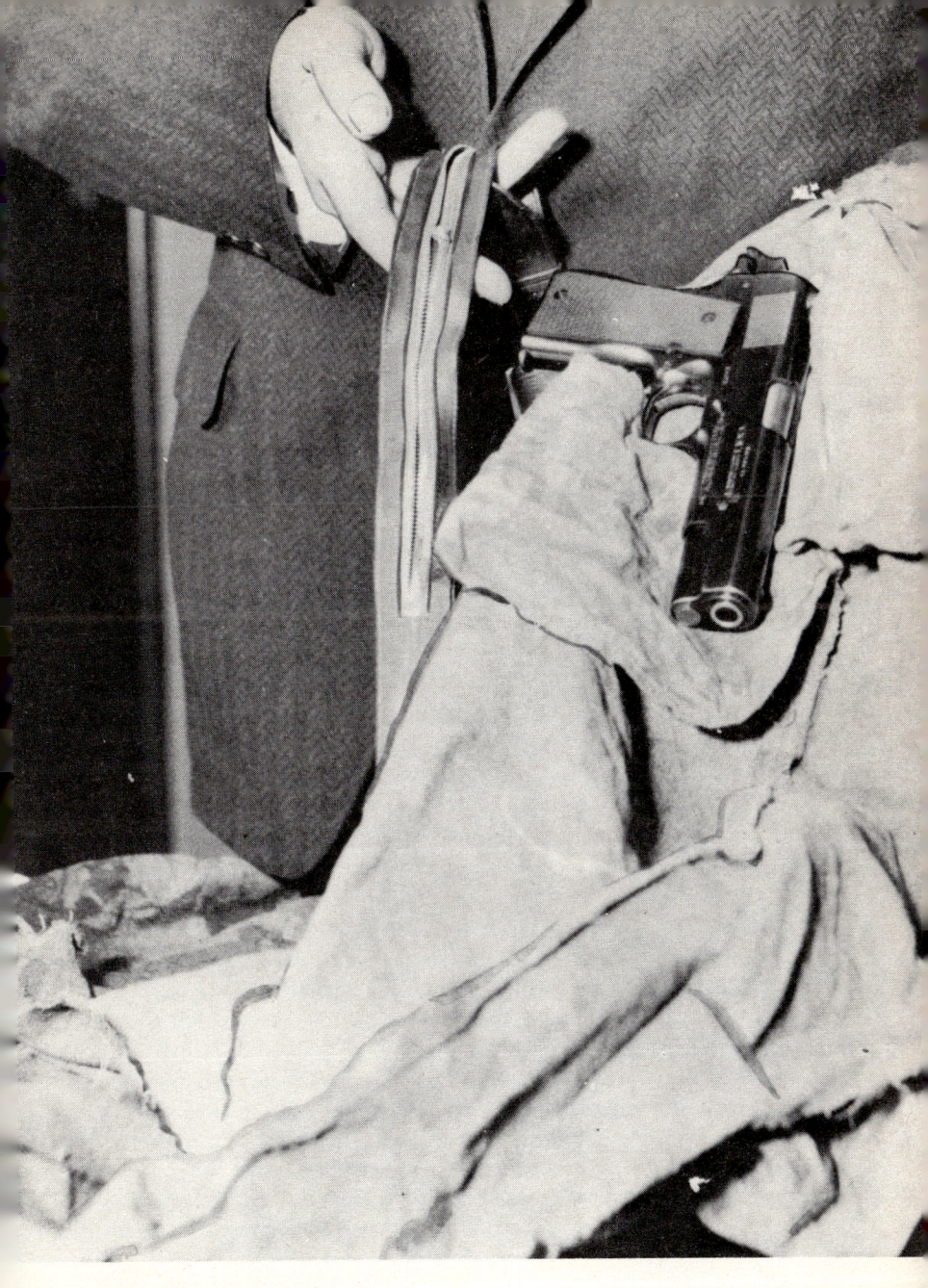

Nelson's gun, money belt, and bloody clothing. His wife dumped his nude body in a ditch when he died.

The FBI maintained that Nash arranged the escape of eleven prisoners from the penitentiary at Lansing, Kansas—the same prison Karpis had made the receiver of stolen goods (clothing). After the escape, Nash found it convenient to take his bride on a honeymoon. They wandered around awhile before returning to Hot Springs. FBI agents were waiting. They picked him up as he sat swilling beer at a local gambling joint and hustled him out of town by car.

A lot of crooks got excited as friends in Hot Springs manned telephones and spread the word that Nash had been captured. Nash, familiarly known as "Jelly," was quite popular and a lot of people owed him favors. Several attempts to organize rescues were made, but the special agents got Nash safely to Fort Smith where they put him on a train to Kansas City.

It was Verne Miller, a former partner of Nash, who got the chance to be a hero. According to the FBI he went to Johnny Lazia for help. Lazia was at that time the operating director of the rackets in Kansas City—rackets bossed by Tom Pendergast. But of Pendergast, a political power in Missouri, the FBI said nothing. (It was left to the Intelligence Division of the Internal Revenue Service to get Pendergast just as three decades later it got Vice President Spiro Agnew on tax evasion charges.)

Allegedly, Lazia put Miller in touch with two free-lance guns who had just come to town: Adam Richetti and Charles "Pretty Boy" Floyd. Plans were made to rescue Nash at Union Station next morning when presumably he would be switched to a car for the trip to the prison at Leavenworth.

All worked well at first. The train came in on time. Nash was hustled upstairs to the street where a car waited. Seven men guarded him—special agents and police. Waiting in a parked car were the would-be rescuers. As Nash was put into the car, his friends moved in. When the officers disobeyed a command to raise their hands, the outlaws opened up with submachine guns. Since only Miller was personally acquainted with Nash, it isn't surprising that the stream of bullets squirting from two guns made no distinction between cops and crook. Nash was killed and so were four other men—three cops and one special agent. Two special agents were wounded. The seventh man escaped unhurt by dropping to the floor of the car and allowing other bodies to hide him.

It was June 17, 1933, and "the Kansas City Massacre" was

history. More than anything else, it turned the tide of public opinion against all latter-day Jesse Jameses, and made life much harder for Alvin Karpis and all his ilk. Miller, who had Chicago syndicate connections, was "rubbed out" by the Mob five months after the "massacre"—presumably because he was too hot. Floyd was killed in a fight with police and FBI agents near Clarkson, Ohio, on October 22, 1934. Richetti was arrested the day before Floyd died, and was executed in the Missouri gas chamber four years later. By then Director Hoover was boasting that crime doesn't pay. He would have been more accurate, perhaps if he had said: "Disorganized crime doesn't pay."

The increase in the casualty rate made it harder for surviving professionals such as Karpis to find competent help when needed. There were still plenty of men around. The Justice Department in 1936 said crooks outnumbered carpenters four to one and doctors twenty to one. "Everybody wanted to be a crook," Karpis put it, but not everyone had the moxie to be successful. Take Elmer Higgins, for instance.

Higgins came to Karpis's hotel room one day to apply for a job. The men were talking it over when the tough town marshal dropped by to question Higgins about something. Playing dumb, Higgins agreed to go down to the station with the marshal if he could go to his room and get his cap. Karpis smiled, knowing Higgins had a rifle in the room. He prepared for action. But then Higgins came back—wearing his cap. Off they went. Recovering from his astonishment, Karpis went after the rifle, chased down the marshal and his prisoner on the street, disarmed the marshal, and took him back to the hotel room and tied him up. Only then did he discover that Higgins's rifle wasn't loaded.

Sparing no words, Karpis declined to accept the volunteer as a member of his gang. Undisturbed, Higgins went out on his own a few days later and tried to rob a drugstore. The druggist fired back. Both men died.

But finding good men wasn't the only problem. Finding something worth stealing became increasingly difficult as the Depression deepened. Karpis even raided Coffeyville, Kansas, in search of loot. Times had changed since the day the Daltons came to grief there. Karpis and his men got away untouched, but their loot—from a shoe store, pool hall, drugstore, and gas station—totaled only $150.

NELSON'S REIGN AS ENEMY NO. 1 LASTS 128 DAYS

Was Lured by Crime Trail When Only 13.

For exactly 128 days George [Baby Face] Nelson bore the title No. 1 public enemy of the nation. He succeeded to the title when John Dillinger was slain and kept it until he was shot to death Tuesday by the federal agents who were also slain in the battle.

Baby Face, whose real name was Lester M. Gillis, was 25 years old. He was branded as the "most desperate criminal" because he was a merciless killer, a quick trigger man with an insane hate of "coppers and G men." He was an expert with a machine gun, with the cowardly nerve necessary to shoot in the back.

Nelson, although known as Baby Face because of the cherubic pink of his cheeks and his slight stature—he was five feet four inches tall and weighed 133 pounds—did not have the disposition the name implies. He was surly, cruel. Agents who sought him say he had no friends.

Feared by His Pals.

Two men seized with him in 1931, after a series of bank robberies, holdups, and burglaries, told police he was "a killer at heart." They said they were always in fear of him.

His crime career began at 13 when he was caught stealing auto accessories and sent to St. Charles School for Boys. He was intelligent enough to become a model prisoner, thus escaping punishment. Twice he was

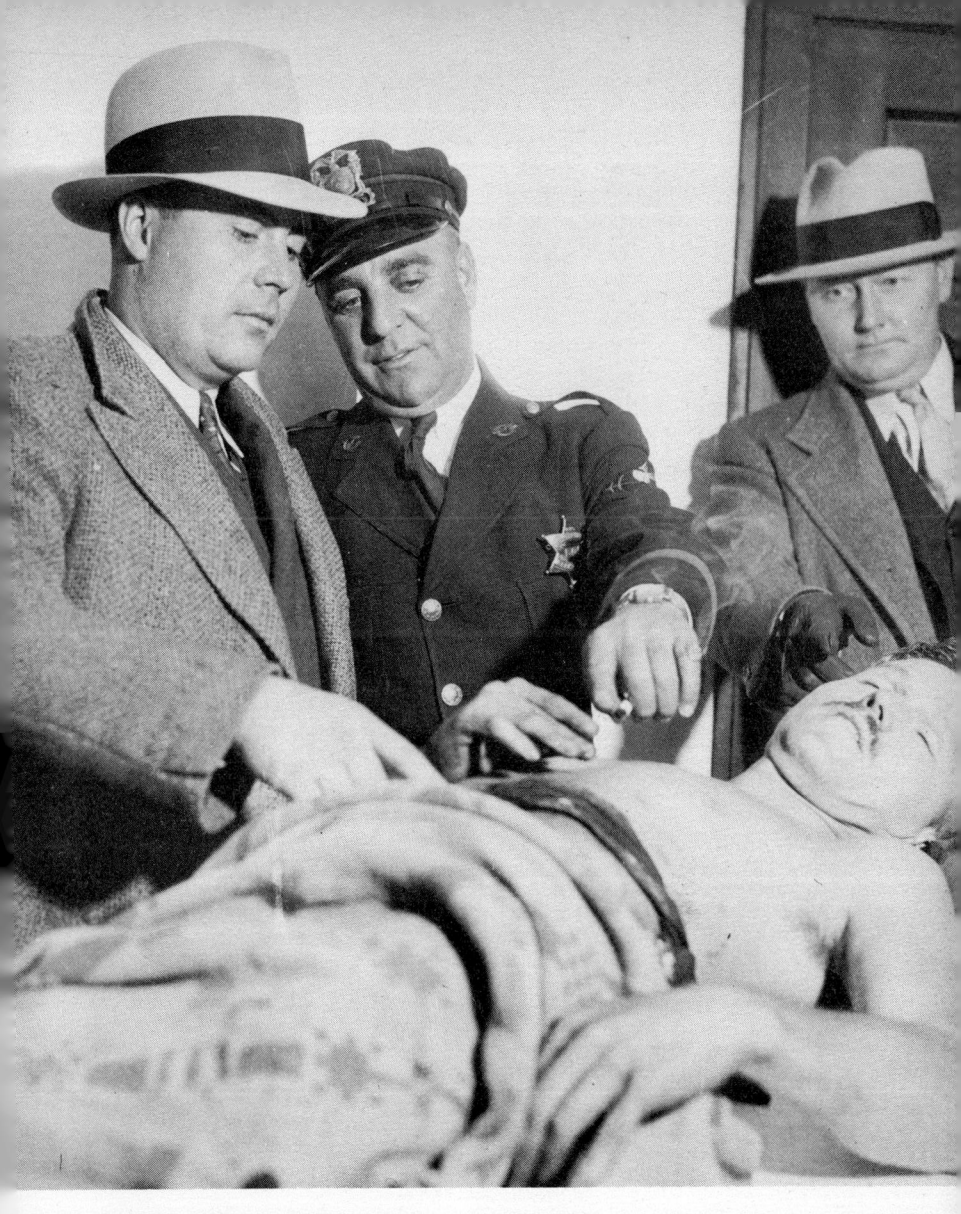

Nelson's body on slab at Niles Center, Illinois. The day before this picture was taken he was involved in a shootout with federal agents, two of which were killed. They found seventeen slugs in his body.

It was this type of reward as much as anything that made the Karpis-Barker Gang turn to kidnapping. They went into it with eyes open, knowing that the FBI would assume jurisdiction instantly. The target chosen was William Hamm, Jr., a bachelor and the president of a brewing company in St. Paul. Beer with an alcohol content of 3.2 per cent had just become legal and business was booming. Hamm, the gang decided, wouldn't have much trouble raising $100,000 ransom.

All went well. Hamm proved most cooperative, and Karpis kept him supplied with reading material and beer. One slight change of plans was made after the operation began. The ransom was originally to be delivered by one of Hamm's beer trucks. Word came, however, that the cops were going to put a machine gunner under the tarpaulin on the truck, so new orders were sent specifying the use of a stripped-down Chevy with all doors removed.

The money was picked up, Hamm was released with his wallet untouched, and the Karpis-Barker Gang began waiting out the "heat" before spending the money. Their streak of good luck continued when the Touhy Gang had an automobile accident up in Wisconsin. A highway cop came along and ordered them to follow him to the nearest police station. In all innocence Roger Touhy obeyed. A search of the car revealed some guns, handcuffs, and adhesive tape, all of which was enough evidence for Director Hoover to announce that the Touhy Gang was responsible for the Hamm kidnapping. Months later the Touhys won acquittal, but by then the Karpis-Barker Gang had spent the Hamm loot and moved on to other things. Some of them weren't productive.

Shotgun George Zeigler, an old crony, came up with what appeared to be a sure thing. He had noticed that every weekday evening just before midnight, a messenger with two armed guards rolled a loaded pushcart from the main post office in Chicago down the street to the Federal Reserve Bank. It was easy to assume the pushcart was loaded with cash. Why not hit it and make a really big score? he asked.

Karpis planned the caper, even to having a second car equipped with a smoke-screen device parked on Jackson Boulevard to enable the getaway car to get away under cover of the smog. At the last minute, however, he dropped out and let the Barker brothers and three others handle it. Everything worked perfectly, including the smoke screen, until they had a perfectly normal wreck when another car forced them off the road. Hustling, the men stopped a passing Buick, loaded the stolen mailbags into it, and took off. But the Buick was low on gas. They had to stop, steal another car, transfer the mailbags again. In addition to being dangerous, it was a lot of hard work. Finally, however, they made it to their hideout and started opening the bags. Checks and nothing but checks. They were worthless. And to get them they had lost a specially equipped car and the diamond had fallen out of Doc Barker's ring.

It was enough to make a man turn honest. Well, almost enough. Instead, the Karpis-Barker Gang pulled its second kidnapping, snatching Edward Bremer, a St. Paul banker. The ransom was eventually paid—$200,000 in bills whose serial numbers were recorded. The money was hot, and it got hotter as the reaction began. President Roosevelt discussed the crime in a radio chat from the White House, and the FBI—with a chance to gain new glory—flooded the midwest with special agents. Even the money changers in Reno who would ordinarily exchange hot money at a discount refused to touch the Bremer ransom.

To fill up the slack, Karpis went to work for the operators of the Harvard Club in Cleveland as "muscle," and did such a good job he was given a small interest in the profits and a cottage in which to live with his pregnant girlfriend. Apparently Karpis, who liked to boast he was a thief and not a syndicate hoodlum, didn't realize that the Harvard Club was a gambling joint controlled by the Cleveland Syndicate. It had been taken from its founder, Frank Joiner, put on a businesslike basis by the syndicate's casino troubleshooter, Sam "Gameboy" Miller, and turned over to Shimmy Patton and Art Hebebrand to operate. As a casino, it was little more than a big barn and not to be compared with the plush places the syndicate operated in Kentucky, Las Vegas, and Havana in later years. Nevertheless it won a claim to fame as the place Eliot Ness tried to raid on January 10, 1936. The former "Untouchable" of Chicago fame was Cleveland's Safety Director. Responding to a call for aid from a newly elected reform prosecutor, Ness led thirty-three cops to the scene. By the time he arrived the club had been stripped of gambling equipment and the raid achieved nothing but headlines. The syndicate

St. Paul Dispatch

ST. PAUL, MINN., SATURDAY, JUNE 17, 1933.   HOME EDITION   PRICE TWO CENTS IN ST. P

RD FROM HAMM KIDNAPERS WAITE

Sankey Denies Husband Has Part in Ca

KILL
BUSH
AS CITY

HOME OF KIDNAP VICTIM; TWO OF HIS SISTERS

SAFETY OF MILLIONAIRE
ABDUCTION VICTIM TIE
HANDS OF ST. PAUL PO

St. Paul Dispatch

Sometimes it is the most valuable in Contract, says expert. Read Ely Culbertson's article on this topic on Page 10 today.

ST. PAUL, MINN., WEDNESDAY, AUGUST 30, 1933.   HOME EDITION   PRICE TWO CENTS IN ST.

SLAIN, ANOTHER SHOT IN $30,000
OUTH ST. PAUL MACHINE GUN RA

VICTIMS AND SCENE OF PAYROLL ROBBERY

1 OF 5 BANDITS BELIEVE
WOUNDED BY POLICE
AS BATTLE RAGES IN S

Confronting ck Messengers as T don't supply Patri warns on Page 10 to-day.

St. Paul Dispatch

ST. PAUL, MINN., THURSDAY, JANUARY 18, 1934.   TWO CENTS IN S

W. G. BREMER KIDNAPED
$200,000 RANSOM ASKE

ABDUCTION VICTIM, KIN AND KIDNAP SQUAD

Secrecy Vei
Second Ma
Seizure He

Victim Member of One of St. Paul's Wealthi
Son of Adolph and Nephew of Otto Bremer
Manager of Home Owners Loan Company
Call Gave Tip

VANISHED AFTER TAKING HIS DAUG
TO SUMMIT SCHOOL ON GOODRIC

Edward G. Bremer, president of the
State bank and a member of one of St.
families, was kidnaped for $200,000 ran
morning.

soon regained control and gambling resumed at the Harvard Club and a dozen others. By then, of course, Karpis was no longer interested.

That ransom money was still burning a hole in the pockets of the Karpis-Barker Gang. Someone suggested it could be exchanged in Cuba—at a fifteen percent discount. The money was dug up—the boys hadn't used Mason jars and it had gotten wet—dried out, and taken to Miami. There Karpis stored his submachine guns at Biscayne Kennel Club—a dog track controlled by the syndicate—and went on to Havana by boat. The country was controlled by Fulgencio Batista, an ex-sergeant who had seized power the year before. Batista was even then being courted by Meyer Lansky who would soon emerge as boss of gambling, but at that time Havana was still something of an open city and even thieves were welcome if they had money. Karpis settled down to stay awhile and enjoy the sun, but after a few weeks some of the Bremer money popped up in circulation and shortly afterwards the FBI arrived in force. Florida seemed suddenly attractive, the more so since Freddie and Ma Barker had settled down in a cottage on the shores of Lake Weir, southwest of Ocala in the rolling hill country of central Florida.

For Karpis the cottage, with its orange trees and small boat, was paradise, but after a short visit he went south to Miami and rented a house in the Little River section—then and now a favorite hangout for hoods. Fishing was the order of the day, Back at Lake Weir, however, hunting suddenly became popular.

Unknown to Karpis in Miami, and to Freddie at the lake, Arthur "Doc" Barker had been captured in Chicago. For one reason or another—smart detective work or third-degree methods—he had revealed the whereabouts of his brother. The FBI moved quickly. Special planes brought in the troops and during the night of January 16, 1934, they slipped into position. As the sun came up, they assaulted the cottage with machine guns, high-powered rifles, and tear-gas bombs. There was some return fire but soon it ended. When the sound of birds singing could be heard again, the FBI agents entered the cabin to find Fred Barker dead with fourteen bullets in his body. Ma Barker was also dead. Hoover later claimed she had taken part in the battle and was the devil incarnate, the mastermind of the Karpis-Barker Gang. Well, some justification is needed when you shoot an old woman. At least the Pinkertons didn't call Jesse James's mother the mastermind of the James Gang when they blew off her arm in a night attack on her home.

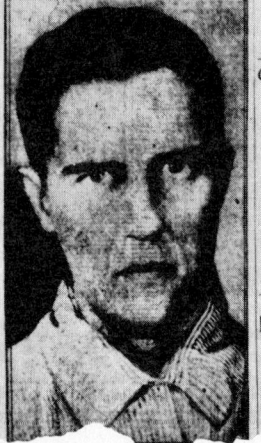

Karpis was out fishing when the news broke, but he lost little time getting out of town upon learning about it. With him was an old friend, Harry Campbell. Someone at the dog track steered them to Atlantic City, a corrupt resort city on the coast of New Jersey. It was a bum steer. Shortly after arriving they were trapped in a hotel room. In the gunfire that followed, Karpis's mistress was hit in the thigh by a stray bullet and abandoned as the two men fought their way out to a car. Things got hairy for a few hours but they made it to safety.

There was still enough elbow room to pull a few jobs. One was a mail truck containing the payroll for the Youngstown Sheet and Tube Company. The loot was $72,000. Karpis considered taking his share and checking out for Australia, but, as always, there was one last job he wanted to do. As he put it:

"I'd been mulling it over for weeks. I was going to take a mail train. I thought of the great bandits of the Old West, the James Brothers, the Dalton Boys, and all the rest of them. They knocked over trains, and I was going to pull the same stunt."

So there you have it.

The plot called for the train carrying payrolls from the Fed-

Opposite page, the New Orleans newspaper report of the capture of Alvin "Creepy" Karpis, seen at center of above photo. Hoover (*left foreground*) leads the way as Karpis is taken into federal court in St. Paul, Minnesota.

eral Reserve Bank in Cleveland to the steel cities of Youngstown, Warren, and Niles. The area was a breeding ground for gangsters and in years to come the scene of a bloody war between Mafia factions for control of the barbut game (a multiple-dice game). But Karpis, as Public Enemy Number One, was getting more attention than all the hoods of Youngstown combined.

Despite one member of the gang dropping out because of an attack of gonorrhea, the robbery went pretty much as planned. Karpis had to toss some sticks of dynamite around before convincing the clerks in the mail car he was sincere, but he got the goods. There was just one hitch—the payroll for Youngstown had been shipped the day before. The loot came to only $34,000. Karpis consoled himself, however, with the thought that he had duplicated the feats of "the famous old western bandits."

The smallness of the score kept him from leaving the country as planned. He had to try again. Meanwhile, the heat kept him moving through the remainder of 1935 and into 1936. Hot Springs again offered sanctuary, but even it wasn't safe for long. The handwriting was on the wall, but Karpis refused to believe it. With the easing of the Depression, moods had changed. The G-Men were the new heroes of America and were working hard to increase their prestige.

Early in May, 1936, they captured their quarry in New Orleans. Alvin Karpis walked out of a house in shirt sleeves, carrying no gun. Squads of FBI agents closed in as he climbed into a car. Director Hoover was there in person, an honor Karpis could appreciate. No one had troubled to bring along handcuffs—an indication Old Creepy wasn't expected to be taken alive—so his hands were tied together with a necktie.

Back at FBI headquarters, Hoover called Karpis a hoodlum. Karpis objected.

"I'm no hoodlum," he said. "I'm a thief."

He went on to explain that a hoodlum or hood sold himself to organized crime and took pay for killing people. A thief, on the other hand, was an independent operator who worked at his trade. Hoover didn't understand the distinction.

Almost thirty-three years later, after spending twenty-five of those years at Alcatraz, Karpis was paroled and deported to his native Canada. He emerged without apologies, without regrets. He had, after all, survived.

Alvin Karpis on a shopping spree, his first in thirty-two years, after his release from McNeill Penitentiary in Washington state. He was paroled on the condition that he be deported to his native Canada. He is seen here buying a Valentine's Day gift for his sister, who still lives in the United States.

Joseph J. "Specs" O'Keefe "sings" to a grand jury six years after the robbery and a short time before the statute of limitations could be applied to the case. He said he talked because he didn't get his share of the money.

6

Impossible Dreamers

MIDCENTURY BOSTON WAS corrupt, misgoverned. So was metropolitan Miami in the 1960's. But what had these conditions to do with the careers of Joseph F. McGinnis and Jack "Murf the Surf" Murphy? Or, to be more specific, what had they to do with the Brink's robbery and the theft of the Star of India?

So long as the possession of material things is the prime measure of ego satisfaction, just so long will men confederate in gangs to achieve their goals through the freest of free enterprise.

* * *

Joe McGinnis was born in 1903 in Providence, Rhode Island. His father was a tough Irish cop. His sickly mother was a gentle soul who had hoped for a daughter she could baby. Stubbornly she refused to accept biological fact and Joe wore dresses and long curls for his first nine years. Then his mother died of tuberculosis.

Now in trousers, Joe finished grade school and found a job as a hotel bellhop. As a means of learning about human nature, the job has to rank with that of errand boy for whores and gamblers. As a matter of fact, about the only difference was the bellhop's uniform.

Joe's father had lost his natural affection for Joe back when Joe was acting like Josephine, so he made the break complete by sending his son to South Boston to live with an older brother. South Boston was a rough neighborhood then, and it hasn't improved much with age. Joe found a home with the Kneeland Street Gang which operated in the vicinity of South Station. At age seventeen he had the dual experience of being shot by a cop (not seriously) and being sentenced to the reformatory. Upon getting out Joe headed back to Rhode Island, where he became a boxer, perhaps in an effort to impress his tough old man. It was a good idea but, unhappily, Joe was unable to impress anyone, especially his opponents, in the squared circle. It seems that someone had drafted rules. Joe liked only his own rules. Soon he was in the state prison for burglary. When he got out he returned to Boston where people had a more tolerant attitude.

Joe met an enterprising madam up on Beacon Hill. She was just the right age—young enough to be attractive and old enough to be smart. He married her and she set him up with his own speakeasy. Boston was serviced by Rum Row during Prohibition's latter stages. Charles "King" Solomon was the big wheel, until the syndicate bumped him off for getting illusions of grandeur, and a lot of men laid the foundations of their fortunes—men such as Joseph Linsey and Joseph McGinnis.

All went well until 1938 when Joe was given a short vacation in Leavenworth for transporting narcotics. He claimed it was all a mistake—he didn't know the guy he was riding with was hauling the stuff—but his wife divorced him, nevertheless. She was generous, however, and demanded no settlement or alimony. All of which suited Joe fine when he got out of prison. He bought an old speakeasy near Egleston Square in the central part of Boston and named it the "J.A. Cafe." A liquor store was added next door and there Joe ruled in turtlenecked glory. (He was fond of turtlenecked sweaters long before the jet set realized they made men look masculine.)

From this headquarters Joe assembled a select group of thugs and assigned them various jobs. Again, membership was not fixed, not constant. Men were employed according to the demand of the assignment and their special qualifications. Nor was there a pattern in the enterprises they engaged in. Joe pictured himself as the mastermind, the Big Brain, and delighted in thinking up off-beat capers. He married one of his bar girls and assigned her to operate the liquor store. A stripper who showed executive ability was put in charge of running the saloon. He couldn't marry her but she had free access to his bedroom. Naturally, the two women didn't like each other but they competed vigorously to make money for Joe and to satisfy his physical whims. Joe, naturally, considered himself quite smart to have devised such an efficient arrangement.

A Napoleon needs an army. Joe had his choice of an international cast: Greeks, Chinese, Syrians, Irish, Jews, and, of course, Italians. Boston was full of punks—from thieves to syndicate gangsters. No one ethnic group dominated although many gangs formed along ethnic lines. In Boston, the fabled "Melting Pot of American Democracy" had failed to work properly. Perhaps it had been overloaded around the turn of the century.

Tony Pino, three years younger than McGinnis, was one of the inner circle. He ran a diner in partnership with his brother-in-law, Vincent Costa, and as Pino followed McGinnis, Costa followed Pino. A fat man, Pino was something of a Jackie Gleason in his ability to inspire laughs. He was the comedian of the gang. Costa was the dude, the fop, but he was also considered one of the best "wheelmen" in Boston. He knew how to get around the crowded, narrow streets of that unplanned city. A third "regular" was Michael Geagan, the best educated of the gang. He had actually gotten into high school before entering the business. His friends valued his courage—if that is the word for it—more than his accomplishments in the classroom. Mike was fearless, afraid of no one or nothing. Then there was Adolph Maddie, better known as "Jazz the Bookie." He liked loud clothes and loud music and wandered around the bars of South Boston setting up drinks and collecting bets. Thomas Richardson and James Faherty were known as the "Gold Dust Twins." They always stuck together, in prison or out, and were generally considered both cool and tough. Joseph Banfield was known to like the bottle a little too much, but when sober he was an expert on burglar alarms and other protective devices. He was also a good wheelman. Youngest of all —only twenty-nine in 1947—was Stanley "Gus" Gusciora. As a boy he had operated his own juvenile gang and had ended up in reform school. While trying to escape he murdered a guard and served seven years in prison, then joined the Navy during the war. He was considered reliable and a friend of Joseph "Specs" O'Keefe. An outsider was O'Keefe, but he had such a reputation that when any burglary showing signs of intelligent planning was committed, he was automatically picked up and questioned.

Even today not too much is known about the mental processes that made McGinnis decide to pull the world's biggest robbery. It is clear, however, that a long string of successful jobs up to 1947 gave him tremendous confidence and even greater ambition. He took no part in the actual robberies, preferring to appear in his tavern at the time of the crime, but all of them were planned to the last detail in his backroom. Typical was the robbery of the American Sugar Refining Company plant in Revere on October 30, 1947. Revere was a snydicate-controlled resort city just north of Boston. The masked bandits escaped with $29,000. They struck again next day, hitting a factory in the southern part of town and getting the payroll—$107,999 in small bills.

It was enough to swell the ego. And, if the evidence is correct, McGinnis began planning the Brink's robbery even as the loot was being counted.

In December, Pino approached O'Keefe about taking part in a "big job." Cautiously, O'Keefe wanted details. Pino wouldn't give them. It was in January, 1948, that a second contact was made. This time Pino listed a lot of names—but he did not mention McGinnis. Specs knew the gang as professionals. He accepted. Only then did Pino disclose the target. It was in September, after a summer of planning, when McGinnis revealed himself as the Mastermind-in-Charge. He was welcomed aboard.

McGinnis planned no part in the robbery itself. He was to remain in his cafe, conspicuous by his presence, on the night of the robbery. He would earn his share by taking care of all the loot until it could be safely divided, and by supplying alibis as needed for the others. Besides, it was all his idea in the first place.

Complicating planning in the early days was news that

Left, some of the money left behind by the gunmen after tying up five employees of Brink's, Inc., in Boston. *Far left*, employees working in the vault area.

Brink's planned to move to a new location in the North End of Boston. The new site was on Prince Street and that fact is ironic. Fifteen years later when it became fashionable to blame all crime in Boston, past and present, on the Mafia, the local headquarters of that overrated organization was on Prince Street. Had the crime taken place in 1963 instead of 1950, the Mafia could have been the whipping boy. As it was, Boston police refused to believe local talent could pull such a sensational coup and sought evidence that an out-of-town gang was responsible. Getting a lot of consideration was the legendary Purple Gang of Detroit which had ceased to exist in 1933.

After Brink's moved into its new quarters, the robbers began dropping in uninvited. The visits were made at night, utilizing various lock-picking devices to gain entrance. The interior was thoroughly explored. Soon the men could draw maps from memory showing the locations of doors, desks, and furniture. They spent night after night there, studying the layout, seeking the keys to the interior doors and information about the burglar-alarm system. They never found it. They even raided the company furnishing the alarm system in hopes of finding records that would supply the needed data, but to no avail.

Nineteen forty-nine arrived and still the studying, the planning, the exporing went on. The men were in no hurry—the loot was worth the wait. Finally they recruited a new member, Henry Baker, just out of prison and an expert on locks and keys. He suggested they take the locks out of the doorknobs

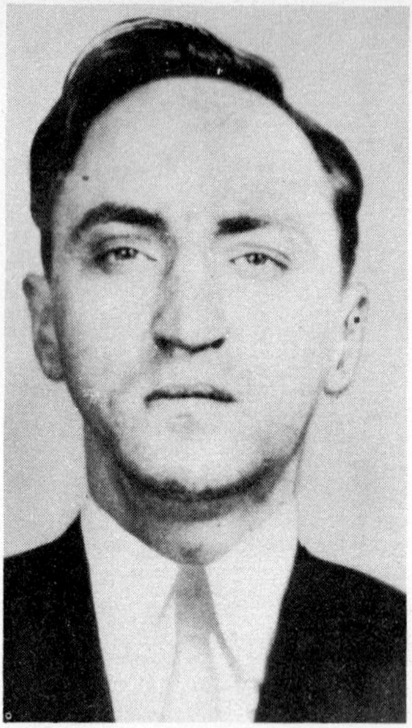
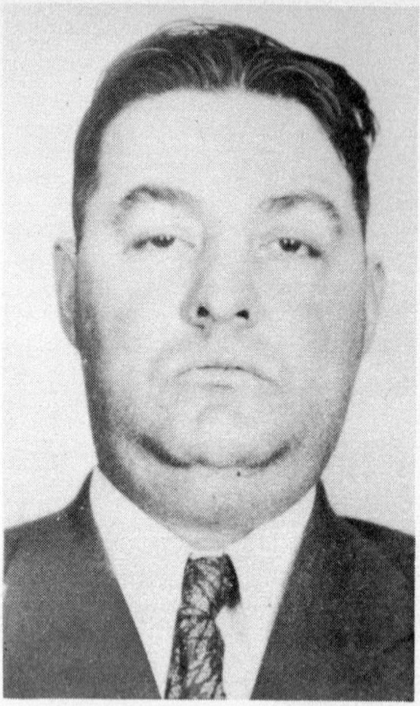
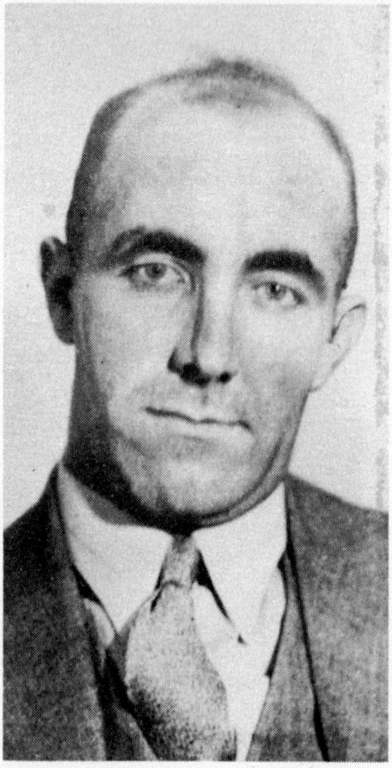
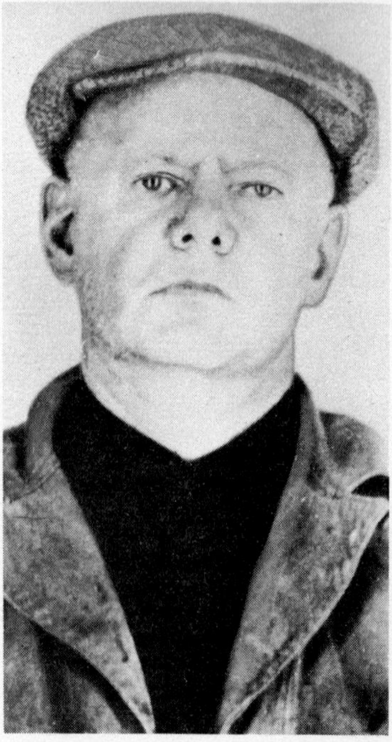

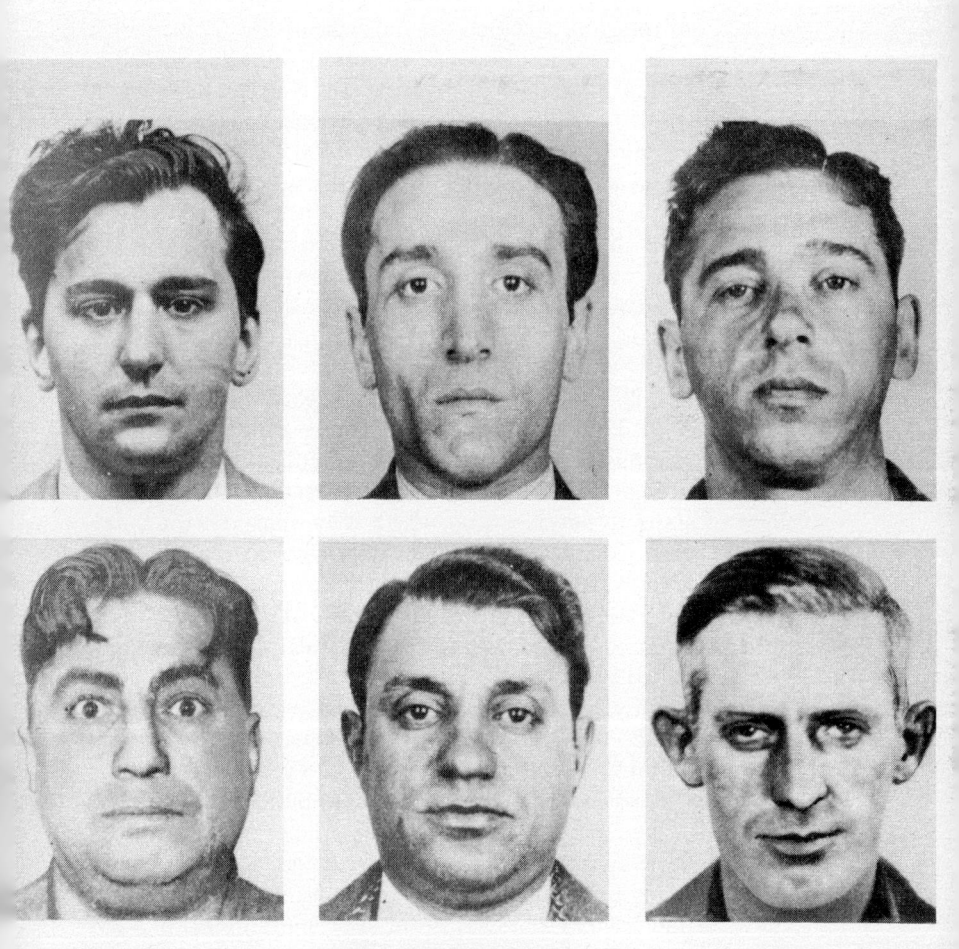

Participants in the Brink's robbery of $2,775,394 in cash, bonds, checks, and securities. *From left; top row*, James I. Faherty, Joseph S. Banfield, Stanley Gusciora, Vincent Costa, Henry Baker; *bottom row*, Michael Geagan, Joseph F. McGinnis, Anthony Pino, Adolph Maddie, Thomas F. Richardson.

and have keys made—and this was done. It took several nights, in fact, but the gang accepted the risks cheerfully. The problem of burglar alarms was ultimately bypassed—it was decided to stage a holdup instead of a break-in. Each night from six to seven-thirty, the vault was open as clerks checked the cash collected that day by the fleet of armored cars. Using the keys, they would invade the building quietly, slip up on the vault and surprise the clerks.

It sounded simple after the months of frustration and everyone agreed it was the best procedure. There was a lot of work still to do—cars, a truck, guns, and Halloween masks to obtain. Christmas was merry that year and everyone looked forward to a prosperous New Year.

After several false starts, the raid took place on January 17, 1950. Specs led the way. McGinnis, of course, was back at his tavern, generously buying drinks for a police captain. They entered through a side door on Prince Street, went up a short flight of stairs to another door which they opened with a key. Beyond was a corridor and another door into a suite of offices. Two more doors were passed and at last they could peep around a barrier into the open vault. Three clerks were working there, protected by two guards. With drawn pistols, the gang stepped into the lighted area.

Guards and clerks were quickly tied with rope and silenced with adhesive tape. With almost no conversation the gang proceeded to do what it had trained for two years to do—transfer the bags and hampers of cash from the building to the waiting truck. They overlooked a mobile safe holding the $800,000 payroll of the General Electric plant, but they still moved out half a ton of money in seventeen minutes. And they left no clues behind—either physical or in the minds of Brink's employees.

They took the truck to the designated house—home of Jazz the Bookie's parents who knew nothing about the caper. In a back room they counted the money, segregating ten $1,000 bills and $88,000 in new bills as too dangerous to spend. Discarded also was a millian and other securities—much of it easily stocks, bearer bonds, and other securities—much of it easily convertible. But the counting process grew boring after a while and it was left for Brink's accountants to come up with the official total: $2,775,395.02. Of this, only a quarter of a million was in nonnegotiable checks and commercial paper. Actual cash totaled $1,218,211.19, which made it by far the largest cash haul in history.

As previously mentioned, local police didn't want to credit Boston-area badmen with such a colossal caper. This reluctance was in line with the prevailing philosophy among officials in every city where a certain amount of illegal activity was winked at on the grounds that it filled the vacuum which otherwise would be filled by syndicate gangsters who wouldn't be satisfied with crumbs when the whole cake was available. One man given much consideration was Willie Sutton, a modern genius at getting into banks and out of jails.

"Slick Willie" was famous for his use of uniforms: mailmen, telegraph messengers, policemen. Presumably the desperate officers in Boston thought the gargoyle masks used by the Brink's bandits might be a variation of that technique. Sutton, of course, was accustomed to getting the blame. After his successful robberies of the early thirties gave him fame, his name came up automatically whenever police were baffled or reporters needed an extra angle. When in 1934 a former Follies beauty, Gertrude Wlliams, killed herself, newspapers noted that in happier days Willie Sutton robbed her home of $50,000 worth of jewelry, and after that, alas, it was all downhill for Trudy.

Try as they might, however, the police couldn't tie Sutton into the Brink's caper. Nor did anyone else fill the bill. Despite hundreds of tips, some from nuts and some sincere, police were—to use an appropriate cliché—baffled. So was the FBI, although it never admitted it. Presumably, the robbers could have met at a convenient location, divided up the swag, and vanished happily into oblivion. That this didn't happen is the responsibility of Joe McGinnis. He had masterminded the largest cash holdup in history, and now his ego developed a new ambition. Why not keep all the cash for himself? It will be remembered that McGinnis's contribution to the robbery was his promise to secure the money in a safe place until it could be divided. Well, somehow he had managed to do it. Only McGinnis knew where it was hidden, and he was in no hurry to tell.

Meanwhile, Specs O'Keefe began to wonder if McGinnis wasn't deliberately directing attention his way. A gun taken from Brink's was found near his home. Then the cut-up truck used in the robbery was located near O'Keefe's residence.

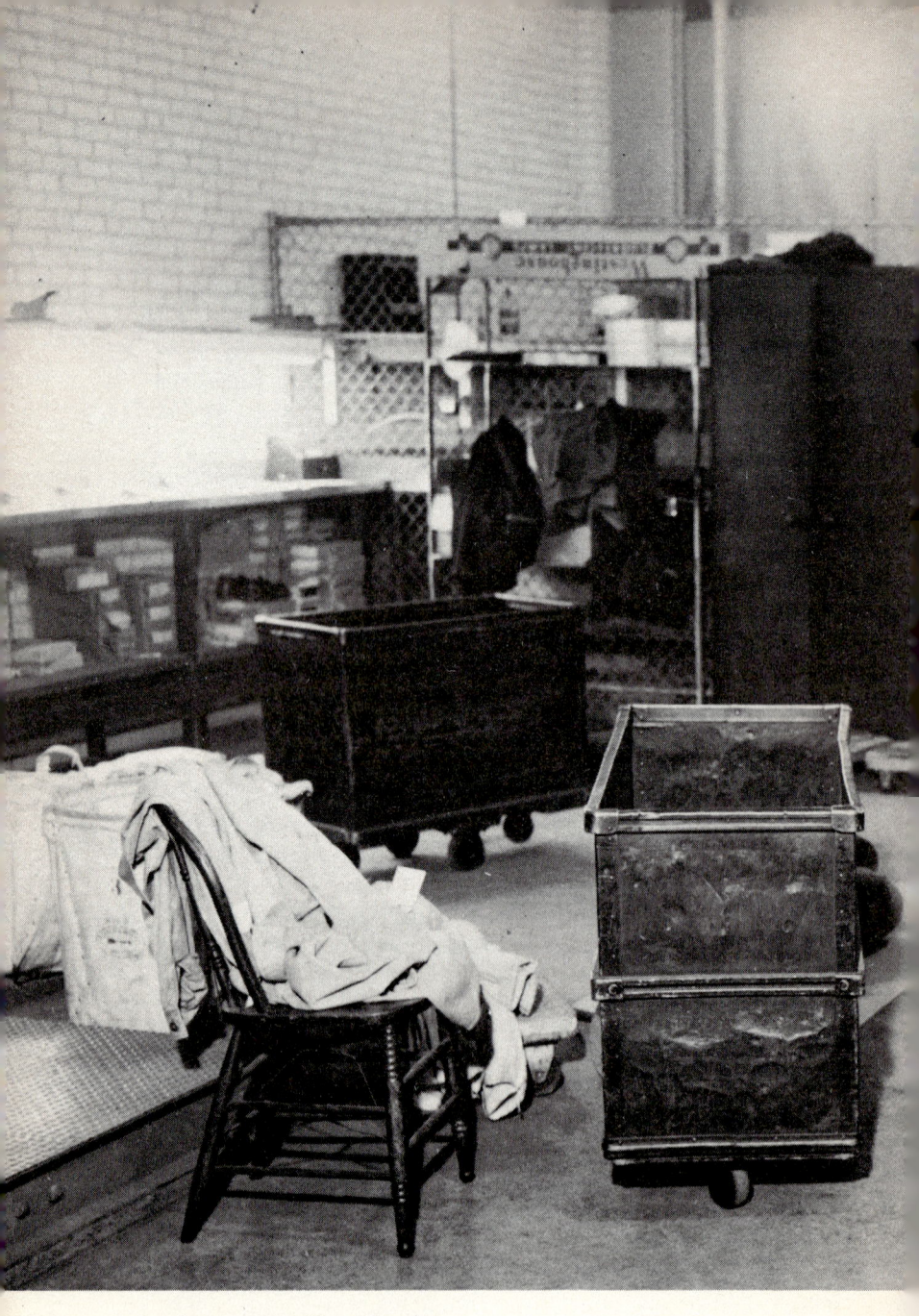

A police reconstruction of the crime using Brink's employees, showing how they were tied and forced to lie on the floor.

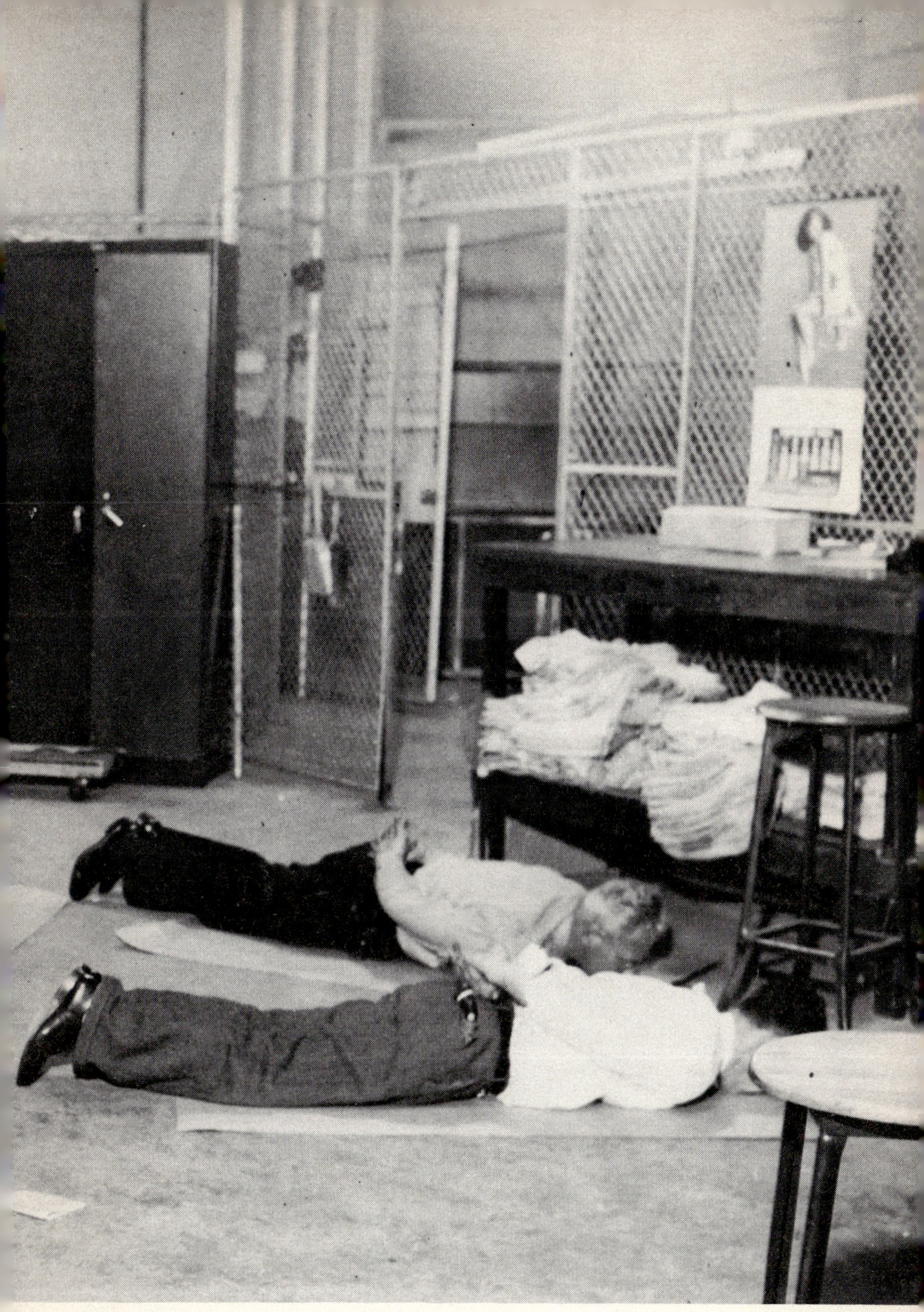

Twice he was picked up and questioned. As the only real suspect, he had to be extremely careful in everything he said or did. Perhaps the thing to do was get out of town until the heat cooled. His pal, Gusciora, agreed, and suggested they go to St. Louis where he wanted to visit the grave of a brother killed in the war. Specs had $5,000, taken from the loot for pocket money, so away they went.

The FBI was on their tail all the way. Operating on the theory that Specs was enroute to visit the Brink's booty, special agents watched their every move. It was rather disappointing, and perhaps boring. Several weeks passed. The men were returning eastward when the FBI lost the trail on June 7. After a few hours of panic, someone figured out the two men were headed home. There was one logical route—across northern Pennsylvania, southern New York, and into western Massachusetts. Police agencies along that route were alerted to be on the lookout.

Specs and Gus drove cheerfully along, planning the showdown with McGinnis that seemed necessary, and taking time out to steal some revolvers in Kane, Pennsylvania, and some suitcases down the road in Coudersport. In the town of Towanda they were recognized. Chief Don Meredith proved to be a man of agility—he charged them with stealing a lawnmower that had been reported missing earlier in the day. The charge permitted him to secure a search warrant, and the stolen guns were found in the trunk of the car. Now there was something more solid on which to hold these men who were suspected of pulling the biggest heist in history. And despite his share of the loot—allegedly waiting in Boston—Specs had great difficulty getting his friends to put up bond, pay lawyer's fees, etc. He and Gus remained in jail as months went by.

Meanwhile, someone pulled another job to startle the imagination. An armored car was robbed in Revere of $681,000 in small, used bills. They did it in broad daylight while three

An early arrest photo of "Slick Willie" Sutton, "The Actor," with some newsclippings of his variegated career in crime.

guards were sitting a few feet away having a coffee break. Investigation revealed that the garage where the truck was kept was in the same building housing Brink's. What's more, keys to the car were kept in an unlocked drawer in the building. Obviously someone had duplicated a key and then returned the original to its place. This fact seemed to relate the two robberies. But one seemed as unsolvable as the other.

There was excitement late in 1951 when a small-time punk was arrested and tried to make a deal. He knew the Brink's case was the biggest headache going so he offered to solve it. The mastermind, he said, was a Carlton O'Brien, a nightclub operator and friend of Joe McGinnis. Someone promptly blasted O'Brien with a shotgun, killing him instantly and giving the stoolie's story some credence. Promptly the stoolie improved on it. Reaching wildly, he said that Carlton's co-mastermind was his buddy, Joe McGinnis.

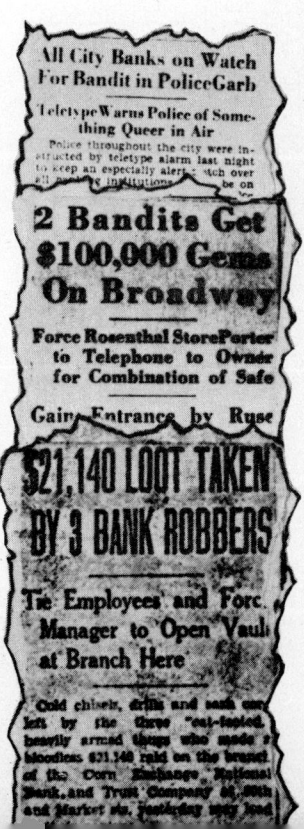

Police picked up McGinnis but his alibi stood up. And soon officers learned the stoolie was in Tampa months before and after the Brink's robbery. Obviously, he didn't know what he was talking about. Why then was O'Brien killed? Perhaps because someone hoped to make a dead man the fall guy.

On January 18, 1953, the federal statute of limitations ran out, but Director Hoover vowed the FBI would keep investigating. Meanwhile, Specs finally got out of jail on bond. He was out long enough to decide he had been double-crossed by McGinnis and to realize that someone—he assumed it was McGinnis—was trying to kill him. Two attempts were made. And then, after a few days, came a third attempt. This time a machine gun was used, a weapon not often seen in Boston since a law making mere possession a crime punishable by life imprisonment had been passed twenty years before. Specs was wounded twice, but neither wound was serious. By some good detective work the shooting was traced to Elmer "Trigger" Burke, a New York gunman who had been imported for the assignment. Burke was captured and held in the Charles Street Jail. There was much speculation that he would talk. Instead, two men wearing hoods and equipped with keys broke into the jail and freed him. It was an escape to rank with Dillinger's performance at Crown Point. District Attorney Garry Byrne called it "incredible and fantastic." Just another example of Joe McGinnis's genius, whispered the underworld. The fact that Burke was soon recaptured and shipped off to New York to stand trial for murder didn't change the opinion.

Specs, however, crossed everyone up. Five days before the statute of limitations expired on the state's case, he confessed. Indictments were quickly secured, and McGinnis was exposed as the big brain behind Boston's crime wave. He seemed to enjoy the publicity.

Ultimately, after a trial lasting months, all the conspirators except O'Keefe were found guilty and sentenced to life imprisonment. Specs, for his services to society, was sentenced to time served and released. He disappeared into limbo, given a new identity by the government in an attempt to protect him. Of the $1,219,000 in cash, less than $100,000 was accounted for. Those in the know assumed McGinnis stashed it away somewhere—along with a lot of other dollars his gang stole. Gave him something to think about on the long winter nights.

* * * *

Here is Jack Murphy as seen by FBI Special Agent Norman Ollestad in the days before Murphy became famous and it was still possible for them to go surfing together off Miami Beach:

"He was harmless enough, and actually reminded me a lot of the surf nuts at home. After the edge of his first impression wore off, his hilarious sense of humor began to grow on me. Apart from his job at the hotel he spent most of his time island hopping in the Caribbean, skin diving and chasing the girls from one vacation spa to the next. The woods were full of them, but heiresses and secretaries—they were all the same to Murphy. And when one of them left him in the lurch, or he ran out of money, he'd just sit down and weave hats for the tourists out of palm fronds. When he'd made enough money he'd move on. At least that's how Murphy told the tale."

This, then, was Murf the Surf—a beach bum, but something more. Around him collected a group of similar-minded young men who prided themselves on their physical shape and mental clarity. The world, as they saw it, was full of hypocrites who considered cheating their wives a great adventure, but who in reality were afraid to get out of their air-conditioned Cadillacs and sit on the beach. In contrast, the "Beach Boys" saw themselves as free spirits, bold adventurers, who knew how to enjoy life and saw no reason why they shouldn't.

Just when Murphy got tired of making straw hats and became a jewel thief isn't very clear. But one thing seems certain—the challenge was at least as important as the loot he expected to obtain.

The loot was nothing to disparage—the market value was placed at $380,000, but the *New York Times* quoted experts as saying the twenty-two gems taken were "priceless" because they were irreplaceable.

Target was the American Museum of Natural History in New York City where the Star of India, the DeLong Star Ruby, and the Midnight Sapphire were on display in the J.P. Morgan Room. The break-in was discovered at 10 A.M., October 30, 1964, and the story was all over the *Times* the next day. In those days, the staid *Times* tried to play down stories of crime and criminals, but this robbery titillated the imagination.

"One of the most daring burglaries in recent history," said the newspaper.

Murf the Surf and Allan Kuhn needed all their agility to swing the caper. They climbed a ladder to a fifth-floor window,

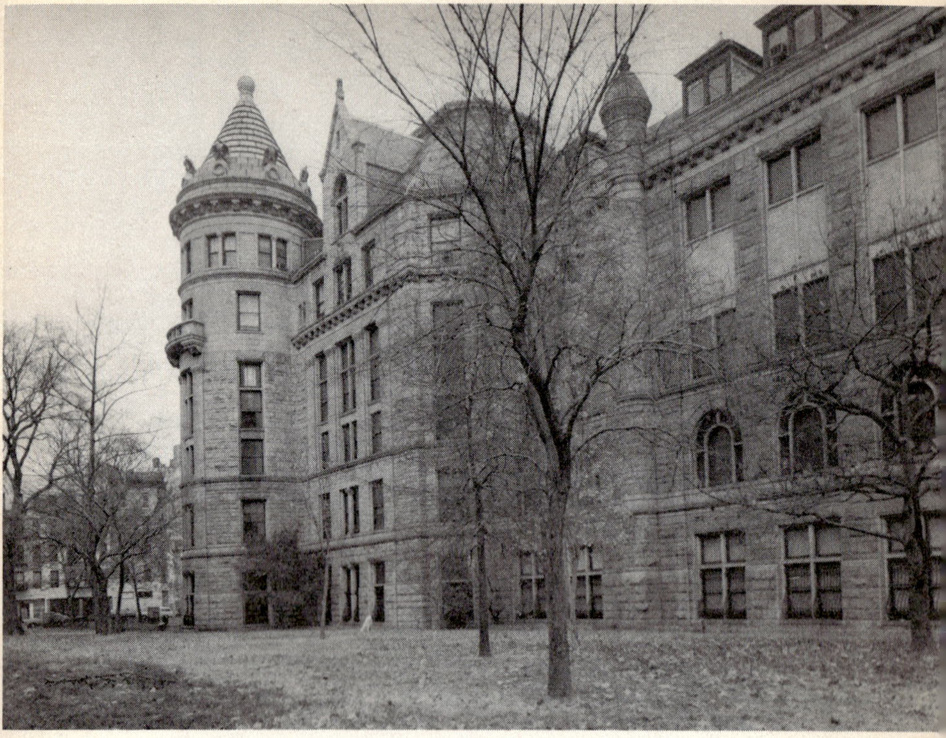

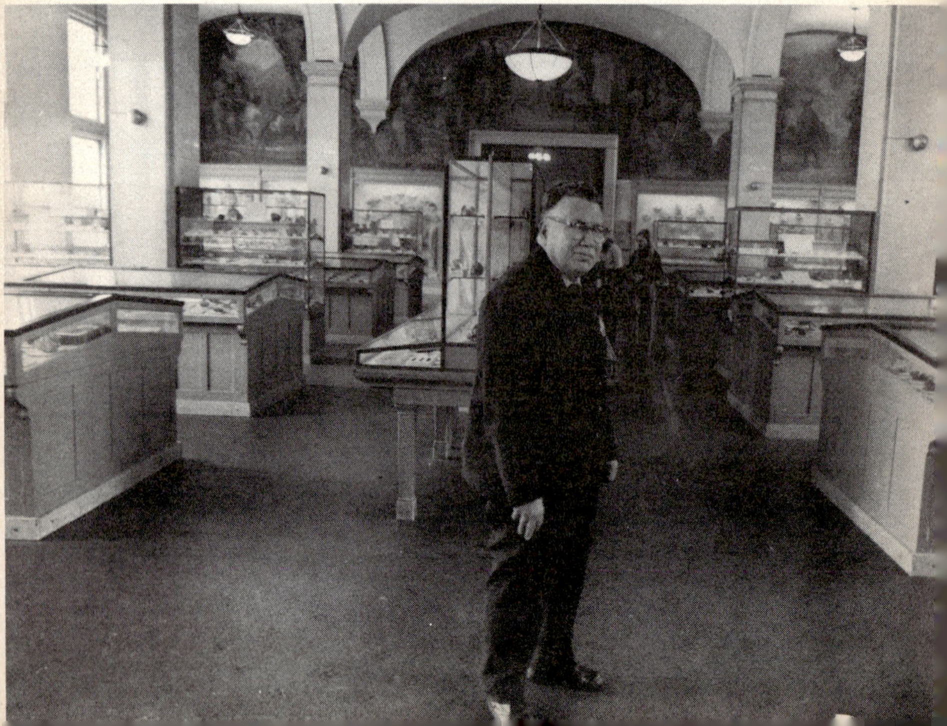

Opposite page: top, the museum battlements scaled by the "Murph the Surf" gang with a ladder, after which they lowered themselves by rope to a fourth-floor window; *bottom,* the J. P. Morgan Room, where the gems were on display. *Above,* the display case *(center)* where they are on exhibit today, with elaborate alarm precautions.

entered the fortress-like building, and swung by rope to the fourth floor where the gems were waiting. Years before, a burglar-alarm system had been disconnected for economy reasons. No guard was on duty inside the room, but one did make the rounds outside at fifteen- minute intervals.

Using a diamond cutter, Murphy cut a circle on the glass above the three major stones after first taping the glass to prevent it from shattering. A tap from a borrowed squeegee and he could lift out the circle and reach in to grab the gems. The Star of India had been donated to the museum by the late J.P. Morgan. It was the world's largest star sapphire, weighing 563.35 carats, and was two and one-half inches in diameter. The DeLong Star Ruby was mined in Burma. The stone reflected a six-pointed star. It weighed 103 carats.

Following the theft, the robbers joined a third man who had been driving a getaway car, and returned to their hotel. Next day they flew back to Miami, leaving the other man to check out at his leisure and follow. The gems were carried to Miami by a nineteen-year-old secretary who had become infatuated with Kuhn during some gay parties at the hotel in the month prior to the robbery. A "fence" was waiting at the airport to take the jewels. Happy to get them, he invited the excited Beach Boys to a party at the $200,000 home of Richard Duncan Pearson—a wealthy yacht broker and gem fancier. The party got out of hand with the arrival of the gems. One young lady in a bikini stuck a gem in her navel and began performing a belly dance. Others followed suit. Finally someone tossed the remainder into the swimming pool and guests had fun diving for them. It was a night to remember.

But alas, someone tipped off the New York cops about the athletic young men who had been celebrating *before* the robbery. The police made a routine check and found the third man in the suite. Unhappily, he had not bothered to dispose of the equipment used in the robbery, and was immediately arrested. There was no code to require him to keep silent if he could help himself by talking so he talked. Thirty-six hours after the burglary, the FBI arrested Murphy and Kuhn.

The jewels, however, had vanished.

In the absence of the booty, federal charges of interstate transportation of stolen goods had to be dismissed. New York officials made it clear that they would be inclined to go easy if only the "irreplaceable" gems were returned. After a lot of complicated bargaining, a deal was worked out. Assistant Prosecuting Attorney Maurice Nadjari went to Miami and eventually recovered the Star of India and eight other gems. But the DeLong Ruby was still missing. Much later, after still more complicated maneuvers, the ruby was ransomed.

Three years after stealing the gems, the Beach Boys were released from prison to face new charges in Miami. They were accused of two other robberies pulled while out on bond in the "big case." The evidence was pretty clear, but such was the state of justice in south Florida in those days that a man could murder his girlfriend, hire some boys to help him dump her body in a canal, and still win freedom on the grounds that he really didn't intend to kill her in the first place. To no one's surprise, Murphy and Kuhn beat the rap.

Murphy enjoyed his notoriety. Shortly after getting out of jail he attended the Easter holiday orgy on the beaches of Fort Lauderdale. Literally thousands of college students flock to town for the holidays and more than half of them are young girls. Murf was the oldest male at twenty-eight—if the narcs be excepted—but the girls found him a real swinger despite his advanced age.

Trouble followed him, nevertheless. In Los Angeles where he went to test the surf, Murphy was arrested along with Kuhn. Officers said they found $2,000 worth of unidentified jewelry, a set of burglary tools, three handguns, and a red-headed woman in their room. The charges were later dropped when the pair got into worse trouble back home.

They tried to go honest. Or so they said. As proof they could point to the surfboard-manufacturing business they set up. But police had their eyes on them and anytime they were spotted in an alley somewhere they were arrested on vagrancy charges. It was all very unfair, Murf maintained.

In December, 1967, the bodies of two young women were found floating in Whiskey Creek off the Intracoastal Canal near Hollywood, Florida, in Broward County, some fifteen miles north of Miami. The women were identified as secretaries in a Los Angeles brokerage firm who were on vacation in Florida. Their stomachs had been slashed open, presumably to release gas so the weighted bodies would sink. For some reason they bobbed to the surface.

When the girls were identified, investigators in Los Angeles revealed they had been seen with Murphy and another of his

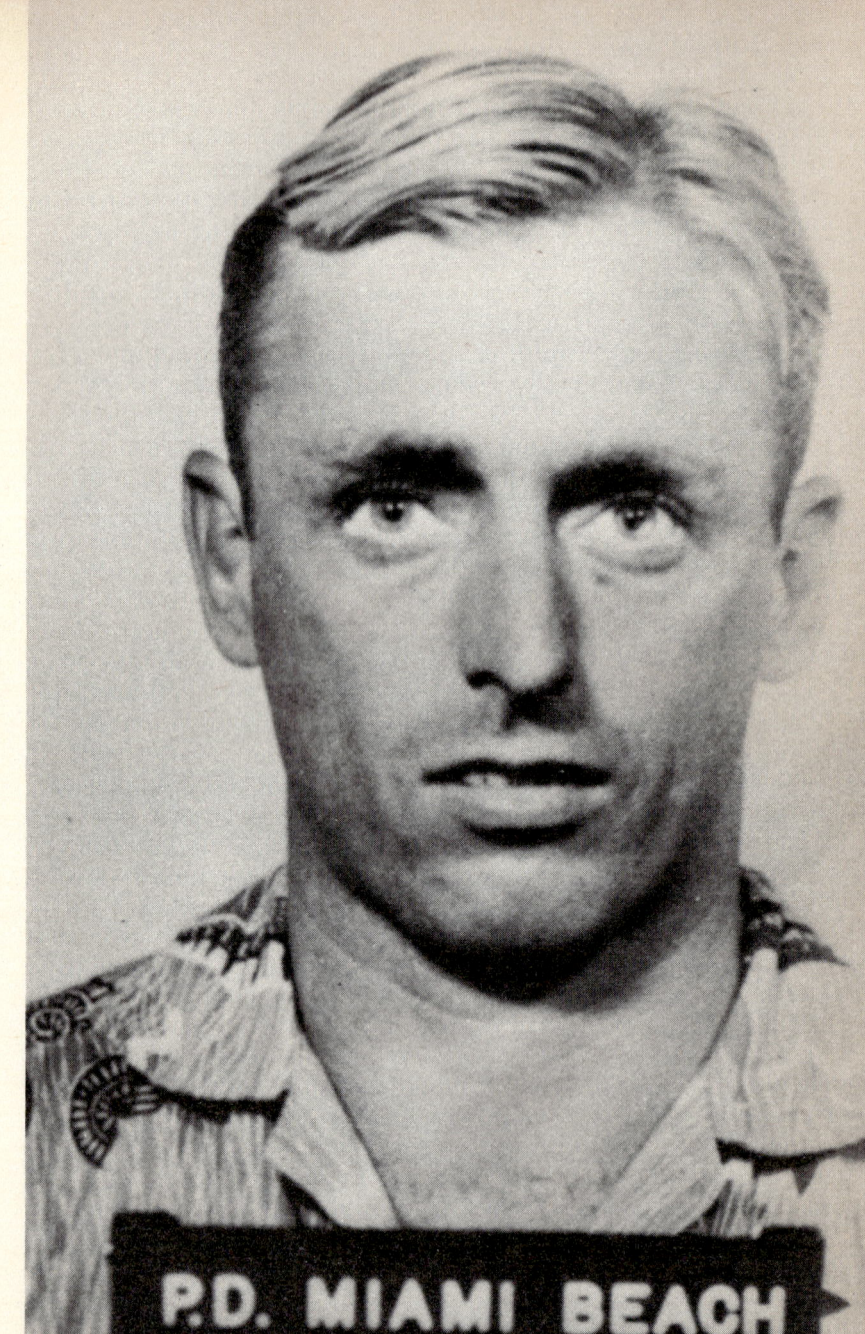

P.D. MIAMI BEACH
A 42203
2 7 64

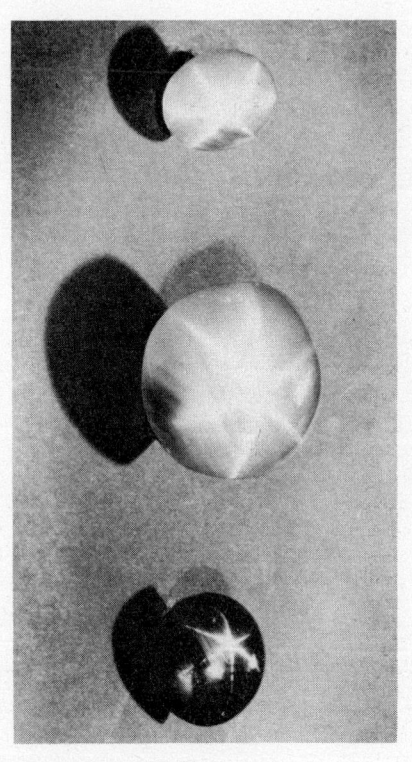

"Murph the Surf" and his gang. *Opposite page*, Jack Rolland Murphy. *This page: top left*, Murphy's co-conspirator, Allan Dale Kuhn; *bottom left*, Roger Clark. *Right*, the three principal jewels stolen: the Edith Haggin Delong Star, a ruby; the Star of India, a sapphire; and the Midnight Star, a sapphire.

associates, Jack Griffith, before going on their vacations. Florida police officials didn't want to believe. Seducing pretty girls, using them, was typical of the Beach Boys—in fact, one of Murphy's girlfriends had killed herself because of unrequited love—but murder was uncharacteristic. Nor could anyone assume it was a crime of passion. Murphy didn't get that deeply involved.

Los Angeles detectives were more cynical, and soon they had a motive. An auditor checked the brokerage firm where the girls had worked and reported that $500,000 worth of securities were missing.

Murphy, meanwhile, and three other men were arrested on January 28, 1968, as they attempted to rob the Miami Beach home of Mrs. Olive Wofford. In the days of open syndicate control, Mrs. Wofford's late husband had nominally owned a hotel bearing his name. She had plenty of clout still. A silent alarm brought police and Murphy suffered cuts when he exited through a closed glass door in a futile effort to escape.

While this was happening, someone discovered a bartender in the Virgin Islands who could testify he was on vacation in Miami the previous December and had witnessed the girls and the Beach Boys depart for Whiskey Creek together. A grand jury indicted Murphy and Griffith on murder charges. Later in the year a federal grand jury charged them with conspiracy in the interstate transportation of a half-million dollars of stolen securities.

In jail with his troubles mounting, Murphy said he wanted to be released on bond so he could hit the lecture circuit and tell people that crime doesn't pay. It sounded funny, but on July 3, 1968, a Dade County judge, Carling Stedman, declared that Murphy was legally insane at the time he pulled the Wofford robbery. The judge, it should be added, won even more fame in 1970 when he directed a verdict of not guilty against Meyer Lansky on drug charges.

During the hearing preceding the insane verdict, a psychiatrist testified that Murphy considered himself a modern Robin Hood. Another doctor quoted the defendant as saying he had been forced into a life of crime in order to pay attorneys and bondsmen. The merry-go-round began, he added, with the Star of India caper.

Stedman's decision created an uproar as everyone, starting with Governor Claude Kirk, elected on a law-and-order platform, got into the act. There was talk of impeaching Judge Stedman. The judge, meanwhile, tried to hold State Senator Robert Shevin in contempt. Shevin, as head of a state crime committee, had made unflattering remarks about the judge.

Meanwhile State Attorney Richard Gerstein—the ineffective veteran under whom Stedman had served before becoming a judge—solved everything by dismissing all pending burglary charges against Murphy in Dade County. For practical purposes, that meant the insanity ruling was moot. Murphy's lawyers promptly got a new hearing in Broward County, but this time the surfer was declared sane. All of which seemed to illustrate the muddled state of law enforcement along the Gold Coast of Florida.

Ultimately, after all the legal delays their lawyers could manage, Murf and Griffith were sentenced to forty-five years in prison for the Whiskey Creek murders. Griffith took it badly and on August 22, 1973, he escaped and got all the way to Phoenix, Arizona, before being recaptured in a hotel room full of rifles, automatic pistols, and one machine gun.

Murphy, however, seemed resigned to his fate. He disclosed he was writing a book about the meaning of it all. Had his old friend and fellow surfer, Norman Ollestad, been present, the ex-FBI agent might have recalled a remark Murphy made on the occasion of their first meeting in the ocean off Cocoa Beach:

"The world's too small a place for the likes of me."

About the Authors

Hank Messick, who did the text for this book, is a specialist in the subject of organized crime. He has written ten books, including four on The Syndicate, the bestseller *Lansky, John Edgar Hoover, The Mobs and the Mafia* (with Burt Goldblatt), *The Private Lives of Public Enemies*, and the recently published *Beauties and the Beasts*, about crime in show business. He was a top investigative reporter for many years, first with the Louisville *Courier-Journal*, where he was actively involved in a campaign to clean up the wide-open city of Newport, Kentucky, and then with the Miami *Herald*. He also studied organized crime in every major U.S. city for two years under two Ford Foundation grants. Mr. Messick lives in Fort Lauderdale.

Burt Goldblatt, who is responsible for the design of this book, has co-authored and designed ten previous books, the latest of which is *Starring Fred Astaire*, a definitive picture-and-text biography. Other books he has designed include *Portrait of Carnegie Hall, The Country Music Story, The Marx Brothers at the Movies, Cinema of the Fantastic, The World Series: A Complete Pictorial History, The Stanley Cup: A Pictorial History*, and *The Mobs and the Mafia* (text by Hank Messick). Mr. Goldblatt is also an artist and photographer whose work has appeared in such publications as *Life, Harpers, Saturday Review, Playboy*, and *Esquire*. In addition, his paintings have been exhibited at the Smithsonian Institution in Washington, D.C. He recently designed and mounted the successful Billie Holiday exhibit at the New York Jazz Museum.

ACKNOWLEDGMENTS AND PICTURE CREDITS

We would like to acknowledge the help of the following people who aided in the research and assembly of this material: First, for their kindness in making their invaluable files available, we thank Mr. William C. Linn and Mr. George F. O'Neill of Pinkerton's, Inc. For additional help in gathering pictorial material we are indebted to Mr. Jack Noordhoorn of Columbia University; Commissioner Robert DiGrazia and Patrolman Bill Trieber of the Boston Police Department; Aram Boyajian, Florence Lewis, and Gene Quattrara of UPI; and Fred Canty of Wide World. We also thank Leslie Goldblatt and Juan Fluhr for help in production, and David Currier for his invaluable editorial assistance.

(Page numbers refer to all photos on a given page, unless otherwise indicated.)

Pinkerton's, Inc.
11, 13, 14, 17, 18, 19, 20, 21, 23, 26, 27, 28, 29, 30, 31, 36, 37, 39, 40, 42, 43, 44, 49, 52, 53, 56, 58, 59, 61R, 63, 65, 66, 68–69B, 73, 74, 75, 76, 77, 78, 79, 81, 82, 85, 86–87T, 106.
Columbia University Library
25, 48, 60, 61L, 68–69T, 71, 86T&B, 87B, 94–95, 98, 100, 101, 103, 104–105T&B, 108, 112, 113, 114–115B, 117B, 118, 135, 137R, 139L, 142, 144T, 148–149B, 153R, 169B, 176L, 180, 182, 199R
Authors' collection
2, 3, 4, 6, 7, 9, 22, 89, 109, 110–111, 116, 117T, 119, 121, 122B, 127, 129, 131, 134, 139R, 141, 144, 145B, 147B, 152–153, 154, 161, 165, 167, 169T, 170, 173, 187, 199L, 200, 202, 203
United Press International
90, 114–115T, 132, 136, 147T, 148–149T, 156, 158, 162, 168, 177, 183, 185, 186, 208R
New York Public Library
8, 12, 34, 35, 45T, 50, 55, 88, 97, 120, 122T, 124, 125, 151
Wide World
137L, 192, 206, 207L
Boston Police Department
190, 191, 196–197
Library of Congress
32, 46, 47
New York City Police Museum
92

Index

Numerals in italics indicate a photograph of the subject mentioned.

Agnew, Spiro T., 174
Alterie, Cowboy, 109
Alvin Karpis Story, The (Karpis), 160
American Legion, 130
Anselmi, Albert, 112, *113*
Atlantic City, 182
Ayres, Tom, 67

Bagnetto, *98*
Baker, Henry, 191, *193*
Banfield, Joseph, 189, *192*
bank robberies, 80, 84
    Dalton Gang, 62, 64, 67, 71
    Dillinger Gang, 126, 130, 133, 143
    James Gang, 9-10, 16, 18, 19, 22, 24, 34-35
    Karpis-Barker Gang, 166
Barker, Arthur "Doc," *161*, 179, 181
Barker, Freddie, 160, *161*, *162*, 164, 166, 171, 181
Barker, Ma (Kate), *158*, 160, *163*, 164, 181
Barker Gang. See Karpis-Barker Gang
Barrow, Clyde, *168*, 172
Batista, Fulgencio, 181
Baum, W. Carter, *142*
Beach Boys, 201, 204, 205, 208
Billy the Kid, 54

Bird, Greenup, 9
Bird, William, 9
Blunk, Ernest, 140
Boone, Daniel, 15
Boston, 187, 188, 189
Bradford, G. A., *40*
Bremer, Edward, 179
Brink's, Inc. theft, 187, 190-200
Broadwell, Dick, 64, 67, *69*, 70
Bryant, Blackface Charley, 57
Buchalter, Louis (Lepke), 160
Buckley, Chris, 95
Bullion, Laura, 84
Burke, Elmer "Trigger," 200
Byrne, Garry, 200

Cagney, James, 110
Campbell, Harry, 182
Capone, Al, 111, 113, 171
Carr, Jeff, *87*
Carver, William, *78*, 84
Cassidy, Butch (Robert LeRoy Parker), 72, 73, 74, 75, 76, *79*, 80, 83, 88, 89
Cassidy, Mike, 80
Chase, John Paul, 171
Cherokee Nation, 57
Chew Tin Gop, 96
Chicago, 110
Chinatown (San Francisco), 91, 93, 97
Civil War, 15
Clark, Roger, *207*

212

Cleveland Syndicate, 171, 179
Cline, Sheriff Frank E., 6, 7
Colosimo, "Big Jim," 93
Connely, Marshal Charles, 70
Cosa Nostra, La, 15, 107
Costa, Vincent, 189, *193*
Cowley, Samuel, 171
crime, 1–2
Crittenden, Governor Thomas, 41, *44*, 49
Crockett, David, 15

Dalton, Adeline (Mrs. Lewis Dalton), 51, 54
Dalton, Bill, 54, 57, 62, *63*, 70–71
Dalton, Bob, 54, *56*, 57, 62, *63*, 64, 67, *68*, 70, 109
Dalton, Emmett, 54, 57, *63*, 64, 67, 70
Dalton, Frank, 54, 57
Dalton, Grattan (Grat), 54, 57, 62, *63*, 64, 67, *69*, 96, 109
Dalton, Lewis, 51, 54, 57
Dalton Gang, 57, 62, *63*, 64, 67, *68–69*, 70, 71
Davis, H., 87
Depression, 159
Dillinger, Audrey (sister), *120*, 121, 143
Dillinger, Beryle (Mrs. John H.), 124, 125
Dillinger, John (father), *120*, 121, 123, 124–125, 145, 146, 155
Dillinger, John H., 2, 62, *120*, *122*, *124*, *125*, *127*, *129*, *132*, *136*, *137*, *152–153*, 171
 bank robberies, 126, 130, 133, 143
 captured, 138
 childhood, *120*, 121, 123, *124*
 death, *148–149*, 151, *152–153*, 154, 155
 Evelyn Frechette, 130
 FBI Wanataka raid, 146, 150
 first robbery, 124–125
 marriage, 123–124, 125
 Navy, *122*, 123
 O'Malley murder, 134
 prison escapes, 128, 140, 143
Dillinger, Mary (mother), 121
Dillinger Gang, 130, *131*, 133, 134, 143

Dimaio, Frank, *106*
disorganized crime, 1, 2
Doolin, Bill, 71
Dyer Act, 143

Evans, Chris, *58*, 62, 94
Evans, Eva, 62

Faherty, James I., 189, *192*
FBI (Federal Bureau of Investigation), 107
 Bremer kidnapping, 179
 Brink's theft, 195, 198
 Dillinger pursuit, 128, 130, 143, 145, 146, 150, 155
 Hamm kidnapping, 178
 Karpis-Barker Gang, 178, 181, 184
 Frank Nash capture, 174
 "Baby Face" Nelson duel, 171
 Star of India theft, 204
Ferber, Edna, 54
Florida, 5
Floyd, Charles "Pretty Boy," *170*, 174, 175
Ford, Charles, 41, *42*, 49
Ford, Martha, 41
Ford, Mrs. (mother), *42*
Ford, Robert, 41, *43*, 49
Frechette, Evelyn, 130, 133, 134, 143, 145, 155
Funk, Si, 87

Gable, Clark, *151*, 155
gangs, 2. *See also* tongs
Geagan, Michael, 189, *192*
Genna, Angelo, 119
Genna, Mike, *118*, 119
Genna, Tony "the Aristocrat," 112, 119
Genna Gang, 112, 113, *114–115*, 119
Gerstein, Richard, 209
Gillis, Helen, 171
Gillis, Lester. *See* Nelson, George
Glispin, Sheriff James, *40*
godfather concept, 107
Gong, Eddie, *90*
Graham, Bill, 171
Graham, Harold, 130

Griffith, Jack, 208, 209
Gusciora, Stanley "Gus," 189, *193*, 198

Hamer, Frank, 172
Hamilton, John, *131*, 134
Hamm, William, Jr., 178
Harlow, Jean, 110
Harris, Sidney J., 2
hatchet man, 93
Havana, 181
Hebebrand, Art, 179
Hennessy, David, 99, *100*, 102
Heywood, Joseph L., 34, 35, 36
Haitt, George, 87
Higgins, Elmer, 175
Hite, Clarence, 16, 41
Hite, Wood, 16, 41
Holley, Sheriff Lillian, *136*, 138
Hollis, Herman, E., 171
Hoover, J. Edgar, *147*, 175
  Ma Barker, 160, 164, 181
  Brink's theft, 200
  Dillinger, 146, 150, 155
  Hamm kidnaping, 178
  Alvin Karpis, 157, 184

Indiana law enforcement, 130
Internal Revenue Service, 174

James, Frank (brother), 10, 15, 17, 22, 29, 30, 32, 33, 38, *47*, 49, 67, 145, 155
James, Mrs. Frank (nee Annie Ralston), 29, 30
James, Jesse Woodson, 2, *8*, *13*, *14*, 17, 29, 32, *46*, *47*, 51, 54, 62, 110, 111
  bank robberies, 16, 18, 19, 22, 24, 34–38
  childhood, 10, *11*, 15
  children, *44*
  Civil War, 15–16
  death, *45*, *46*, *47*, 49
  marriage, 30
  Pinkerton raid, 33
  Robin Hood image, 28
  train robberies, 24, 27, 34, 41
James, Jesse, Jr., 32, *44*

James, Mrs. Jesse (nee Zerelda Mimms), *19*, *29*, 30, 49
James, Reverend Robert (father), 10
James, Zerelda (mother). *See* Samuels, Mrs. Reuben
James Gang, 16, 18–19, 22, *27*, *32*, *34*, 35, 38, 41
Johnson, Payne, 19
Joiner, Frank, 179
Justice Department, 151, 175

"Kansas City Massacre," 174
Karpis, Alvin (Albin Karpowitz), *156*, *165*, 171, 172, 175, 181, *182*, *183*, *185*
  bank robbery, 166
  captured, 184
  childhood, 157
  early career, 159–160
  Hamm kidnapping, 178
  Harvard Club, 179
  Ma Barker, 160, 164
  train robbery, 184
Karpis-Barker Gang, 160, 164, 166, 178, 179, 181
Keele, Polly, 151
Keliher, T. T., *87*
Ketchum, Sam, 83
Kid Curry. *See* Logan, Harvey
Kid Cann Gang, 143
kidnappings, 178, 179
Kilpatrick, Ben (the Tall Texan), *78*, 83, 84
Kirk, Governor Claude, 209
Kloehr, John J., *66*, 70
Kuhn, Allan Dale, 201, 204, 205, 207
Ku Klux Klan, 99

Lansky, Meyer, 160, 181
Las Vegas, 171
Lay, Elza, 72, 74, 75, 76, 80, 83, 84
Lazia, Johnny, 174
Lee, Robert E., 15
Lefores, Joe, *87*
Lem Jung, 96
Liddell, Dick, 41
Linsey, Joseph, 188

Little, Tom, 16
Little Pete (Fung Jing Toy), 91, 94, 95–96
Logan, Harvey (Kid Curry), 79, 81, 82, 83, 84, 88, 89
Longbaugh, Harry (Sundance Kid), 78, 83, 84, 85, 88, 89
Loy, Myrna, 151

McCarthy, Dan, 109
McCarty, Bill, 77
McCarty, Tom, 77
McCarty Gang, 80
McElhanie, Bill, 57
Macheca, 98
McGinnis, Joseph F., 187, 188, 189, 190, 192, 194, 195, 199, 200
McGuire, Andy, 16
McKay, Jim, 171
McKenna, Alexander, 64
McNutt, Governor, 146
Madden, Owney "the Killer," 172
Maddie, Adolph "Jazz the Bookie," 189, 193
Madsen, Marshal Chris, 64
Mafia, 93, 94, 99, 107, 191
Manhattan Melodrama (film), 151, 155
Manning, Anselm R., 37
Marchesi, Sr., 98
Marchesi, Jr., 98
marijuana, 7
Matranga, Charles, 99, 103
Matranga, Tony, 99, 102
Meredith, Chief Don, 198
Merlo, Mike, 113
Miami, 187
Miller, Clel, 34, 35, 39, 41
Miller, Sam "Gameboy," 179
Miller, Verne, 174, 175
Mimms, Zerelda. *See* James, Mrs. Jesse
Monastero, 98
Moore, Eugenia, 56
Moran, George "Bugs," 110, 118, 119
Morgan, B. F., 124, 125
Morton, Nails, 109
Murder, Inc., 160
Murphy, Jack Rolland "Murph the Surf," 187, 201, 204, 205, 206, 208, 209
Murphy, Captain W. W., 40

Nadjari, Maurice, 205
Nash, Frances, 172
Nash, Frank "Jelly," 170, 172, 174
National Guard, 130, 143
Nelson, George "Baby Face," 139, 141, 143, 144, 145, 146, 150, 171, 177
Ness, Eliot, 179
Newcomb, Bitter Creek, 57
Newman, Paul, 88
New Orleans, Parish Prison slaughter, 103, 104–105, 106
newspaper wars, 109
New York Times, 201
Ngin Hoo, 97
Nixon, Richard M., 121, 157

O'Banion, Charles Dion, 108, 109, 110, 111, 112, 113, 119
O'Banion, Viola, 108, 111
O'Brien, Carlton, 199, 200
O'Keefe, Joseph J. "Specs," 186, 189, 190, 194, 195, 198, 200
Ollestad, Norman, 201, 209
O'Malley, Officer William, 133, 134, 138, 151
omerta, 15
opium dens, 91, 93
organized crime, 1, 2

Parker, Bonnie, 168, 172
Parker, Robert LeRoy. *See* Cassidy, Butch
Patton, Shimmy, 179
Pearson, Richard Duncan, 204
Pendergast, Tom, 174
Peterson, Henry, 164
Pierpont, Harry, 131
Pinkerton National Detective Agency, 33
Pino, Tony, 189, 190, 192
Pitts, Charles, 34, 38, 39
Place, Etta, 84, 85, 88, 89
Powers, Bill, 64, 68, 70
Politz, 98, 103
Pomeroy, C. A., 40
Prohibition, 110, 188
Provenzano, Joe, 99, 102
Provenzano, Peter, 99, 102
Public Enemy (film), 110
Purple Gang, 191
Purvis, Melvin, 146, 150, 151, 155

Quantrill, Charles, 9, *12*, 15, 16
Quantrill's Raiders, 10

Rafferty, John, 27
railroads, 28, 62
Ralston, Annie. *See* James, Mrs. Frank
Redford, Robert, *88*
Reno Gang, 24
Rice, Ben M., *40*
Richardson, Thomas, 189, *193*
Richetti, Adam, 174, 175
Rogers, Annie, *81*, 84
Roosevelt, Franklin D., 179

Saager, Edwin, 140, 143
Sage, Mrs. Anna, 151, 155
Sarasota Gang, 3, 4
Sarber, Sheriff Jesse L., 128
Samuels, Archie, 33
Samuels, Dr. Reuben, 10, 16, 33
Samuels, Mrs. Reuben (Zerelda James), 10, 15, *17*, *18*, 182
Scarffedi, *98*
Scalisi, John, 112, 113
Shepherd, George, 16
Shepherd, Oliver, 16
Shevin, Robert, 209
Shirley, Myra Belle. *See* Starr, Belle
Singleton, Edgar, *124*
slavery, Chinese, 93
Solomon, Charles "King," 188
Sontag, George, *58*, 94
Sontag, John, *58*, *61*, *62*, 94
Southern Pacific Railroad, 57, 62
Star of India theft, 187, 201–205
Starr, Belle (Myra Belle Shirley), *50*, 51, *52*, 55
Starr, Pearl (Pearl Younger), 51, *52*, 54
Starr, Sam, 51
Stedman, Judge Carling, 208, 209
Stiles, William, 34, *39*
Sue Yop Tong, 95, 96
Sum Yop Tong, 94, 95, 96, 97
Sundance Kid. *See* Longbaugh, Harry
Sutton, Willie, 195, *199*

Tall Texan, the. *See* Kilpatrick, Ben
tongs and tong wars, 93–94, 97
Torrio, John, *112*, 113
Triest, Germaine, *118*
Tucson, Arizona, 133
Touhy, Roger, 178
Touhy Gang, 178
train robberies, 24, 27, 41, 57, 72, 74
Train Robbers' Syndicate (Wild Bunch), 72, 83, 84, 88

Unione Siciliano (Mafia), 113

Valachi, Joseph, 99
Van Meter, Homer, *131*
Vought, Colonel T. L., *40*

Walker, Joe, 72, 75
Walsh, Coroner Frank J., *152*
Wanatka, Mr. and Mrs. Emil, 146
Weiss, Hymie (Wajiechowski), 110, *116–117*, 119
Wheeler, Henry M., 35, *36*
When the Daltons Rode (Emmett Dalton), 70
Wicher, John W., 31
Wild Bunch. *See* Train Robbers' Syndicate
Williams, Gertrude, 195
Wofford, Mrs. Olive, 208
Wymore, George, 9, 10

Youngblood, Herbert, 140
Younger, Cole, 16, *20*, *21*, 22, *23*, 32, 34, 38, *39*, 41, *48*, 51, *52*, 54
Younger, Henrietta, *23*
Younger James, 16, *20*, *21*, *23*, 33, 34, 35, *38*, *39*, *48*
Younger, John, *21*, 33
Younger, Pearl. *See* Starr, Pearl
Younger, Robert, *21*, *23*, 32, 34, 38, *39*, *48*

Zarovich, Martin, 151
Zeigler, George, 178